Taylor Swift
Love Story

AMY GAIL HANSEN

TRIUMPH
BOOKS

This book is available in quantity at special discounts for your group or organization. For further information, contact:
Triumph Books
542 South Dearborn Street
Suite 750
Chicago, Illinois 60605
(312) 939-3330
Fax (312) 663-3557
www.triumphbooks.com

Printed in U.S.A.
ISBN: 978-1-60078-372-2

Design and page production by Andrew Burwell
Cover design by Paul Petrowsky

Photos courtesy of Getty Images unless otherwise indicated
Photos on page 11 & 16 provided by *Reading Eagle*.

TABLE OF CONTENTS
Taylor Swift: Love Story

INTRODUCTION

Not long ago, Taylor Swift was an unknown country singer trying to make it big in the music industry.

"The first time I heard my song on the radio, I was driving down the road and somebody called in and requested it, and I almost drove off the road – literally," Taylor recalled. "My record label president still has the message of me screaming at the top of my lungs, screeching; you can barely hear what I'm saying because I was crying – it was amazing."

Today, fans do more than simply request Taylor's songs. They buy her albums, attend her concerts, and vote for her for award shows. They've fallen in love with this blonde-haired, blue-eyed cutie. There's no doubt about it; Taylor Swift is a music phenomenon. She was just 16 when she released her first hit single, "Tim McGraw," and less than three years later, she embarked on a sold-out headlining tour. With two mega platinum albums, endless chart-topping songs like "Love Story," and dozens of music awards, Taylor rose to superstar status before she turned 20 years old. Whether she's eating at Cracker Barrel or accompanying her brother, Austin, on a tour of the Notre Dame University campus, Taylor can't go out in public without causing a media frenzy. She's literally everywhere, from *Dancing with the Stars* to *Saturday Night Live,* from the cover of *Glamour* to the video game *Band Hero™.* It seems Taylor Swift proved an age-old theory about success: With hard work, dedication, talent, and a little bit of luck, dreams really do come true.

Perhaps the most character-building, influential time in Taylor's life was her childhood. It was then, at a very young age, that Taylor's personal "love story" began; she fell in love with words and music. Because she had loving, supporting parents, Taylor embraced these interests and honed her musical abilities through live theatre and karaoke. Her childhood was not perfect, however, because Taylor felt like an outcast in junior high school. Feeling left out, Taylor turned to music for support and soon discovered that her personal experiences were good material for honest songwriting. Chapter One, "A Songwriter is Born," details Taylor's childhood in Pennsylvania, her love of music, the heartbreaking days of middle school, and finally a move to Nashville, Tennessee, that changed the course of her life.

Chapter Two, "A 'Swift' Rise to Fame," is the remarkable tale of how Taylor became an overnight music sensation after the debut of her self-titled album. She soon crossed over into the pop music genre and became the first country singer to win an MTV Video Music Award. Her self-titled album and second album, *Fearless,* have both sold millions upon millions of copies, and she was named bestselling artist of 2008. Her quick rise to fame even took the president of her record label, Scott Borchetta of Big Machine Records, by surprise. "What I didn't know was how beautifully this flower would bloom," he said, according to *Country Standard Time.* "People don't just like Taylor Swift, they love Taylor Swift. I am so happy for her. And, she makes all of this so much fun."

So how did Taylor go from unknown artist to mega platinum superstar? Chapter Three, "Secrets of Success," explains how Taylor won over her fans' hearts with honest songwriting. She stood out from her competition by not only singing, but playing the guitar and writing her own songs about things that matter to her fans, like teen angst, romantic love, and heartbreak. She also embraces her fans whole-heartedly. They love her because she makes them feel important. She even keeps in contact with them through MySpace and makes herself accessible at events, concerts, and autograph singings. Because she lives her personal life with integrity, she's also captured the hearts of her fans' parents, who believe she's a positive role model for young women. Perhaps Scott Borchetta summarized Taylor's appeal best when he called her "the full package; somebody who writes her own songs, and is so good at it, so smart; who sings, plays the guitar, looks as good as she looks, works that hard, is that engaging and so savvy," he said. "It's an extraordinary combination."

Taylor also attracts attention because she writes the names of her ex-boyfriends and ex-crushes into her song lyrics. These boys have provided a lot of material for the songwriter, and Chapter Four, "Boy Story," details Taylor's crushes and relationships with ordinary boys as well as famous ones, like Joe Jonas. But Taylor does not spend all of her time thinking about boys. Her friends play an important role in her life, and Chapter Five, "Friends Forever," describes her friendships with other famous female stars, like Selena Gomez and Miley Cyrus, as well as her good friend from high school, Abigail Anderson. It also illustrates the unique friendship she shares with her mother, Andrea Swift.

things that have had the most effect on my life," she said. "But I hope that people who knew me then and know me now would think I haven't changed much. I still drive the same car, still live in the same house, still live in the same neighborhood, still have the same best friend. I don't think I've changed as a person."

Being a country and pop music star, Taylor is often in the spotlight, and she makes sure she always looks her best. Chapter Seven, "A 'Taylor'ed Look," describes Taylor's eclectic fashion sense. From red carpet gowns to sundresses and cowboys boots, Taylor embraces all sides of her personality through her clothes. She even likes to play "dress up" from time to time, especially when she's pranking another country singer.

Taylor turned 20 years old on December 13, 2009, and therefore, is no longer a teenager. What does the future hold for this full-fledged adult? Chapter Eight "All Grown Up" tells how Taylor has already taken on the responsibilities of adulthood. She voted in the 2008 presidential election, designed her own headlining tour, and bought herself a condominium. The chapter also hints at what the future holds for Taylor Swift. A third album? A world tour? Marriage and kids? One thing is certain; Taylor Swift loves her fans, her career, and the life she created by never letting go of her dreams. No matter what happens, Taylor will continue to live her musical life with enthusiasm.

"I'm just so consumed by it," Taylor said of her career. "I'm just so fascinated by every aspect of this. Whether it's radio or videos or concerts, I never want to stop getting excited. I hope I never do."

Taylor's fans love her not only because she's beautiful and talented, but also because she's very down to earth. At heart, Taylor Swift is an everyday girl who likes to pet her cat, Indi, eat at Cracker Barrel and spend the holidays with her family. Even though she's famous, Taylor has gotten star-struck meeting people she admires, like Shania Twain and Rihanna. Chapter Six, "The Real Taylor Swift," proves that stars like Taylor Swift, no matter how famous or how perfect they seem, are real people deep down. Despite her fame, Taylor said she's still the same person. "My schedule has changed, and my age has changed. And those are the two

A Songwriter is Born

CHAPTER ONE: A Songwriter is Born

Taylor Swift's story—a tale about talent, determination, and integrity—begins in southeastern Pennsylvania in the small town of Wyomissing, about 64 miles from Philadelphia. Overall, the weather was mild on December 13, 1989. The temperature averaged 32 degrees, with some fog, snow, and ice. However, this ordinary Wednesday in December marked an extraordinary event. It is the day Scott and Andrea Swift welcomed their first child, Taylor Alison, into the world.

When choosing a name for their blonde-haired, blue-eyed baby, the Swifts picked something androgynous, a name that applies to both men and women. "My mom thought it was cool that if you got a business card that said 'Taylor,' you wouldn't know if it was a guy or a girl," Taylor explained to *Rolling Stone*. "She wanted me to be a business person in a business world."

The Swifts had been successful in business and wanted the same opportunity for their daughter. Scott was a stockbroker, and Andrea enjoyed a career in finance. Taylor's parents valued the corporate world, but they also wanted to provide a peaceful home life for their children. That's why they chose to raise Taylor and her younger brother, Austin, on an 11-acre Christmas tree farm in Wyomissing,

FEARLESS

1. Fearless
2. Fifteen
3. Love Story
4. Hey Stephen
5. White House
6. You Belong With Me
7. Breathe
8. Tell Me Why
9. You're Not Sorry
10. The Way I Loved You
11. Forever & Always
12. The Best Day
13. Change

Behind the Lyrics: "The Best Day"

■ Taylor Swift is known for writing songs about real life experiences, and "The Best Day" from her 2008 *Fearless* album is no exception. She wrote it about her childhood as a tribute to her mother, Andrea Swift. The music video includes original photographs and videos of Taylor Swift as a child with white blonde hair and adorable pigtails.

"It was really cool to go back to that place and reflect," Taylor said. "I wrote some of the lyrics in the song, sort of in a child-like kind of language, which was really fun for me as a writer to stretch that way."

The song describes Taylor's fondest memories, like a cold afternoon at a pumpkin patch and the day her mother set up a paint set in the kitchen. It also depicts a bad day, when Taylor came home crying about the mean girls at school. Her mother helped her through the ordeal. "You hold me tight and grab the keys," she states in the song. "And we drive and drive until we found a town far enough away; and we talk and window shop till I forget their names."

"The Best Day" is about the simple yet meaningful days we spend with our family. In the song, Taylor mentions her father's strength. She also acknowledges her brother, Austin. He is about two years younger and had to grow up in the middle of his big sister's success. "God smiles on my little brother," Taylor says in the song. "Inside and out he's better than I am."

"The Best Day" also expresses Taylor's gratitude for her mother in a less obvious way. Encrypted in the CD jacket lyrics is a secret message: God Bless Andrea Swift.

(See Chapter Three sidebar: How to Decode Taylor's Lyrics)

"My mom thought it was cool that if you got a business card that said 'Taylor,' you wouldn't know if it was a guy or a girl... She wanted me to be a business person in a business world."

A Teacher's Perspective

■ So what do Taylor's former teachers think of her success? Frankly, they're not surprised. According to Sharon P. Luyben, the K-12 Music Department Chair at Wyomissing Area School District, the young Taylor Swift's strengths were "her poise and presence and her ability to write songs."

Sharon first met Taylor when she was 11 and auditioned for *The Sound of Music*. Impressed by Taylor's "amazing" stage presence, Luyben gave her the part of Louisa. "She was very focused and determined to do what she wanted to do," Sharon recalled of the adolescent Taylor Swift. "But she was not obnoxiously competitive; not pushy. Just a quiet leader; a pleasant, wonderful person."

Sharon later taught Taylor in choir. She also interacted with her outside of school. They both attended Bausmen Memorial United Church of Christ in Wyomissing, where Sharon serves as the minister of music. Taylor wrote and performed a song for the church's Christmas program that later appeared on *Sounds of the Season: The Taylor Swift Holiday Collection*.

Songwriting is what truly set Taylor apart from her peers. "Her songwriting skills and creativity are way up there," her former teacher explained.

Taylor's success is largely due to the dedication of her parents, Sharon noted.

She described the Swifts as a nice, normal family. "Her family did everything for her," she said. "They were her promoters and supporters."

In fact, Scott Swift asked Sharon for advice about Taylor's career in music. The teacher recommended Taylor go where country music is popular. "This is not a hotbed for country music," Sharon said of Pennsylvania, "I told him 'If this is the kind of music she wants to sing, she can't stay here. You need to really go where it is.'"

Sharon did not keep in touch with Taylor after she moved to Nashville, but said she's "very proud" of her. It turns out that Taylor is not the only student from Wyomissing to enjoy a successful career in music. Sharon said several of her former students are opera singers or perform on Broadway.

a wealthy suburb of Reading, Pennsylvania. When Taylor was four years old, Andrea left the work force to stay home full time, while Scott commuted to the city for work.

"I know that a Christmas tree farm in Pennsylvania is about the most random place for a country singer to come from," Taylor told *Women's Health Magazine*. "But I had an awesome childhood. We had horses and cats.... Our dad would come home from work and then go outside to make a split-rail fence."

Taylor even had a job on the farm; she checked inside the Christmas trees for praying mantis nests. She participated in many rural activities, like picking pumpkins and learning how to ride horses competitively. This country-like setting turned out to be the ideal place for Taylor to develop her creativity. On the farm, Taylor said she enjoyed "...going anywhere I wanted to in my head."

Words & Music

Taylor showed her creativity at an early age through storytelling. She made up her own fairy tales and in fourth grade, she won first place in a national poetry contest for her original, three-page poem, "Monster in My Closet." One summer, she even wrote a 250-page novel.

"I think I fell in love with words before I fell in love with music," the singer told Katie Couric in an interview. "All I wanted to do was talk and all I wanted to do was hear stories. I would drive my mom insane driving down the road [with her]."

She soon fell in love with music too. She liked to sing with the radio and often entertained her family and herself with songs. Music came easy for her. After seeing a Disney movie, she would walk out of the theater singing all of the songs by heart. Her parents would say, "Didn't you just hear that once?"

Taylor's specific interest in country music developed at age six when she brought home her first LeAnn Rimes album. She was impressed that LeAnn could make music and have a career at a young age. Taylor also liked listening to Shania Twain, Faith Hill and the Dixie Chicks. She believes these women made a positive impact on country music.

"Shania Twain brought this independence and this crossover appeal," Taylor explained. "I saw that Faith Hill, brought this classic old-school glamour and beauty and grace; and I saw that the Dixie Chicks brought this complete 'we don't care what you think' quirkiness."

With so many female role models in country music, it's no wonder Taylor soon felt the urge to sing professionally. That desire may have also been innate, something naturally occurring inside of her, because musical ability runs in her family. Taylor's maternal grandmother, Marjorie Finlay, was an international opera singer who performed in exotic places like Singapore and Puerto Rico.

"I have these gorgeous, glamorous pictures of her all in black and white," Taylor said of her grandmother. "She was just so beautiful."

Her grandmother also sang in church every Sunday. Sitting in the audience, Taylor found the experience both thrilling and inspiring. "I think watching her get up in front of people every single week made me think it wasn't that big of a deal to get up in front of people," she explained.

By age 11, Taylor performed in children's theatre and sang karaoke at festivals and fairs.

Center Stage

At age 10, Taylor wanted to sing before a crowd just like her grandmother, but because she didn't have a band, she decided to perform in musicals with a local children's musical theater company instead. Because she was tall—and looked more like an adult than a child—she often got the lead roles. For example, she played Sandy in *Grease* and Kim in *Bye, Bye Birdie*.

After performances, Taylor attended cast parties, where she discovered another way to perform for a group: karaoke. She enjoyed singing country songs by her favorite female artists. One of her favorite songs to perform was the Dixie Chicks' "Goodbye Earl," which is about a woman who wants revenge on her abusive husband.

Taylor's performances impressed the crowd. "One day, somebody

"One day, somebody turned to my mom and said 'You know, she really ought to be singing country music,'" Taylor recalled. "It kind of occurred to all of us at the same time that that's what I needed to be doing."

Dealing with **Mean Girls**

■ *Mean Girls* may be a movie starring Lindsay Lohan and Rachel McAdams, but dealing with female bullies at school is a reality many teenagers face. Even the beautiful and talented Taylor Swift tried to change her appearance, just to fit in. She often straightened her naturally curly hair because the cool girls at school boasted smooth, straight hair.

"It looked so horrible—it completely frizzed out if it was humid outside, and it took me so long in the morning," Taylor told *Allure*. "But I suffered through that to try and be cool. And when you step out into the real world, you realize that the only place where it's cool to be the same as everyone else is junior high."

Her friends also lied to her. One day, she called several friends and asked them to go to the mall. They all said they were busy or had an excuse. So Taylor went to the mall instead with her mom.

"We ran into all of them hanging out together in a store," Taylor explained. "I just remember my mom looking at me and saying 'You know what? We're going to the King of Prussia Mall!' which is the best mall in the whole state."

Taylor and her mom drove a whole hour to shop at this mall, but it was just the experience to make Taylor feel better.

"We had the time of our lives," she said. "I realized my mom was the coolest person in the world for not making me stay in that mall and suck it up and go on with things. She let me run from my pain for a little bit, and I thought that was the nicest thing that she could have ever done."

turned to my mom and said 'You know, she really ought to be singing country music,'" Taylor recalled. "It kind of occurred to all of us at the same time that that's what I needed to be doing."

Taylor entered karaoke contests everywhere she could, at festivals and the county fair. Dedicated to her newfound hobby, she often pored over the phone book looking for places to sing. Soon, she discovered a karaoke contest at the Pat Garrett Roadhouse in Strausstown, Pennsylvania. The roadhouse owner ran a nearby amphitheater, where traditional country singers performed and still do today. The winner of the karaoke contest got to open up for big stars, like George Jones, Loretta Lynn, and Charlie Daniels.

Taylor proved her dedication and determination by entering the contest every week for a year and half until, at age 11, she won the chance to open for country music legend Charlie Daniels. It wasn't a typical opening act. She sang at 10:30 AM before Daniels' 8:30 PM show.

Taylor didn't put all of her energy and time into karaoke, though. She soon realized that singing the National Anthem was "a great way to get in front of a large group of people if you didn't have a record deal." She started singing the song anywhere she could, even for local garden clubs. She worked her way up to performing the National Anthem at a Philadelphia 76ers game in front of 18,000 fans and later at the U.S. Open tennis championship. It's a song Taylor said gives her "chills," even to this day.

I Want a Record Deal

Around the same time, Taylor watched a TV special about Faith Hill and learned the country star went to Nashville before she made it big in music. Afterward, Taylor bugged her parents constantly about taking her there, and they eventually said yes. Come spring break, her family drove up and down Nashville's Music Row in a rental car

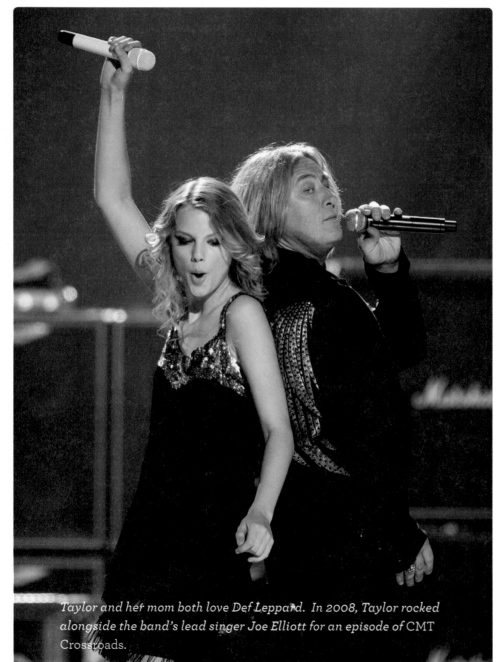

Taylor and her mom both love Def Leppard. In 2008, Taylor rocked alongside the band's lead singer Joe Elliott for an episode of CMT Crossroads.

so Taylor could hand out her home-made demo CDs to receptionists at music labels. Courageously, Taylor would go inside the buildings by herself, leaving her mother and brother to wait in the car. Her pitch was simple: "Hey, I'm eleven, and I want a record deal. Call me.'"

Nashville is full of would-be stars, and Taylor had lots of competition. She came home from Nashville realizing she needed to make herself unique. That's when she started playing guitar and writing songs. "I actually learned on a twelve-string, purely because some guy told me that I'd never be able to play it, that my fingers were too small," she told *Teen Vogue*. "Anytime someone tells me that I can't do something, I want to do it more."

Her twelve-string guitar actually helped her through a very turbulent time. Taylor originally attended the private Wyncroft School in Pottstown, Pennsylvania, so when she transferred to the public school in Wyomissing, she didn't have many friends. The friends she did make soon disliked her interest in unpopular things, like country music. "Anything that makes you different in middle school makes you weird," Taylor told *Rolling Stone*. "My friends turned into the girls who would stand in the corner and make fun of me."

Outcast

Taylor said middle school was a lonely time; she often felt like an outcast. "There were queen bees and attendants, and I was maybe the friend of one of the attendants," she explained. "I was the girl who didn't get invited to parties, but if I did happen to go, you know, no one would throw a bottle at my head."

Meet the Parents

■ No matter her interests, Taylor's parents—Scott and Andrea Swift—were always supportive. "My parents empowered me from day one," she said. "Literally, if I wanted to be something, they honestly believed that I could be."

Taylor's father grew up in Pennsylvania, while her mother's childhood was much more exotic. Her father was an engineer who built oil rigs in Southeast Asia, while her mother was an international opera singer.

"My mom was always stuck sitting backstage somewhere or sitting in a front row, watching a performance..." Taylor said of her mother's childhood growing up overseas. "She thought that when her mom stopped performing, she was relieved of those duties, but all I wanted to do was sing, ever since I was born, so she's always been backstage."

Taylor's mom eventually moved to Texas when she was ten. She was a different child than Taylor. "All my mom wanted to do was ride horses. She didn't want to have anything to do with music," Taylor told Katie Couric. Her mother may have had different interests—in fact, Andrea Swift liked metal bands like Def Leppard over country music—but she served as an excellent role model for Taylor.

"She totally raised me to be logical and practical," Taylor said of her mom. "I was brought up with such a strong woman in my life, and I think that had a lot to do with me not wanting to do anything halfway."

While her mother provides friendship, her father brings laughter. Scott Swift is known for his wacky sense of humor. At one of Taylor's concerts, he rode a Segway scooter around the parking lot and handed out guitar picks with Taylor's picture on them.

"He is the king of one-liners, so he has about 50 million pieces of advice," said Taylor of her stockbroker father. "He'll say, 'Buy bonds!' instead of 'Bye-bye!'"

Andrea Swift raised Taylor to be "logical and practical."

At age 14, Taylor and her family loaded a moving truck to further her country music career in Nashville, Tennessee.

Her parents were well aware of her social mishaps. "After school, I'd hear what nightmare had occurred that day, what awful thing was done to her," Andrea Swift explained to *Blender*. "I'd have to pick her up off the floor."

To fit in, Taylor tried out for school teams but found she wasn't good at sports. Her guitar soon became her best friend. She played four hours a day and couldn't stop. "I would literally play until my fingers bled; my mom had to tape them up," Taylor said. "And you can imagine how popular that made me: 'Look at her fingers, so weird.'"

The popularity contest took its toll on Taylor. She got "dumped" by a popular group of girls; when she would sit down at the lunch table, they would move their trays to another table. They even called her naturally curly hair "frizzy." Feeling left out and confused, Taylor could have turned to drugs or alcohol, but instead she poured all of her attention and emotion to music.

"I used to sit in the back of class and watch these people and their interactions and really wish that I could be included," Taylor told *Blender*. "Part of it was that they were already starting to party at ages 12 and 13—and I was playing at singer-songwriter nights every weekend instead."

Her bad experiences inspired many of her early songs. Writing music was therapy for Taylor. Whenever she felt sad or happy, she would write a song. Doing this helped build her self-confidence. "Those girls could say anything they wanted about me, because after school I was going to go home and write a song about it," she said.

Because she was still mastering the guitar and the art of songwriting, Taylor's first songs were very basic. Some had only three chords because those were the only chords she knew. Taylor later chose live performance over karaoke because the guitar offered her a very portable sound. Instead of dragging a little karaoke machine around, she would plug in her guitar amplifier at coffee houses and even Boy Scout meetings.

"That really expanded the places where I could play and my abilities," Taylor said, "I played so much that I came a long way in a short period of time."

Inspired by other well-known country singers, like Loretta Lynn, Patsy Cline, and Dolly Parton, as well as Kenny Chesney and George Strait, Taylor improved her songwriting skills. Her family started visiting Nashville more regularly, about once every two months. There, she would perform at open mic nights and concerts. Sometimes, she would even collaborate with local songwriters.

Despite her efforts, she still did not get a record deal. That's because, according to Taylor, the music labels in Nashville thought teenagers did not listen to country music. She was told, "the only people that listen to country music and country radio are 35-year-old females." Taylor didn't believe them, and she kept trying. She continued to drop off her demo CDs to music labels.

She also continued to sing the National Anthem, and it was while singing that famous song at the U.S. Open tennis championship that she caught the attention of Dan Dymtrow, manager for Britney Spears. She signed with him for a period and, eventually, RCA Records showed interest and wanted to sign her to a development deal when she was 13.

"That means they want to watch you," Taylor explained. "But they're not promising to make an album with you—kind of like a guy who wants to date you but not be your boyfriend."

She signed the development deal, but later, when the record label decided to "shelve" her—meaning they would just watch her—she chose to walk away. In the end, they would not grant her the freedom to write her own songs. "They wanted to keep me in development until I was probably about 18. So I walked away from the biggest record label in Nashville," she said. "I figured that if they didn't believe in me then, they weren't ever going to believe in me."

Nashville, Here We Come

RCA Records may not have believed in Taylor, but her parents certainly did. They knew that Pennsylvania was not the place to launch a career in country music. To be successful, Taylor needed to live in Nashville, the country music capital. Therefore, in 2004, the family relocated to Hendersonville, Tennessee, a scenic suburb of about 40,000 people that lies north of Old Hickory Lake. Two music legends, the late Johnny Cash and the late Roy Orbison, also called Hendersonville home.

Taylor was definitely the reason for the relocation, but her parents tried not to pressure their daughter about success. "It wasn't like, 'This is your one shot, so make it happen.' They presented it as a move to a nice community," explained Taylor. She said her family loved the friendly people of Tennessee. "If I made something

At the 2009 CMT Awards, Taylor stopped to chat with a young fan.

out of it, great. But if it didn't happen, that would be OK, too."

Because she'd been unpopular in school, the move did not bother Taylor. "Living in Pennsylvania was great, and it was an incredible place to grow up, but I didn't have any friends," she explained. "So I was like, 'Sure, let's move. I'll miss my friends even though I don't have any'... that wasn't a big deal for me."

It was a bigger deal for her father, who had to transfer his work from one state to another. For a while after the move, he commuted back and forth between Tennessee and Pennsylvania. "It was an incredible sacrifice for my parents to make, and I've never forgotten it," Taylor said.

According to her mom, Taylor's love of music and songwriting was at the heart of the decision. "It was

never about 'I want to be famous.' Taylor never uttered those words," Andrea Swift told *Women's Health Magazine.* "It was about moving to a place where she could write with people she could learn from."

Those people she could learn from ended up including renowned songwriters, like Brett Beavers, Troy Verges, and The Warren Brothers.

Before moving to the Nashville area, though, Taylor enjoyed a few early successes. Her original song "The Outside" was selected for a 2004 compilation CD put out by Maybelline called *Chicks with Attitude.* It's an ongoing project that helps young female artists just starting out in the music business. In May 2004, Taylor was featured at a BMI Songwriter's Circle showcase, which took place at a well-known performance venue in

Greenwich Village, New York, called the Bitter End nightclub.

Moving to Nashville ended up being a wise decision. It improved Taylor's already impressive track record as a songwriter and performer. In May 2005, while she was still just 14, Taylor signed a publishing deal with Sony/ATV Music Publishing and became their youngest staff songwriter. Finally, someone wanted to pay her to do something she really loved: writing country songs.

It was her first after-school job, and she took it very seriously. She knew she had to work alongside her 45-year-old songwriting colleagues. "I knew every writer I wrote with was pretty much going to think, 'I'm going to write a song for a 14-year-old today,'" Taylor said in an interview with *The New York Times.* "I would come into each meeting with 5 to 10 ideas that were solid. I wanted them to look at me as a person they were writing with, not a little kid."

Taylor wrote many songs for Sony/ATV, but she preferred to write tunes for her own artistic use. For that reason, she often asked her bosses not to pitch her songs to other artists. "I write them about the guy who's sitting next to me in class, who doesn't notice me," she told them. "And I can't bear to let anyone else sing them."

Moving to Nashville also improved her social life. In a freshman English class at Hendersonville High School, Taylor met red-haired Abigail Anderson. The two girls "bonded" over a discussion about Shakespeare's *Romeo & Juliet;* both of them had negative responses to the play. (This discussion later inspired Taylor to write the hit song "Love Story" and put a positive spin on a very tragic tale.)

"Taylor and I just really connected and, ever since then, we have been inseparable," Abigail said of their friendship.

While attending Hendersonville High School, Taylor continued to write music. She often doodled lyrics in the margins of her school notebooks, which caught her teachers off guard when they conducted random notebook checks. "It's algebra on this side of the page and 'Drew looks at me' on the other side of the page," Taylor joked.

That school year, she wrote the tune "Our Song" for the ninth grade talent show, which later won her best video at the 2008 Country Music Television awards.

Writing and singing her own songs became even more important to Taylor in a city full of young female singers. "I realized...there are a thousand girls who want this just as much as I do," she said. "I figured that I needed a way to stand out, so I got out my twelve-string guitar and started to play my own songs. I figured I wouldn't need to depend on other songwriters."

Lucky Break at The Bluebird Cafe

That decision paid off one fateful night, when Taylor performed at The Bluebird Café in Nashville. There, she caught the attention of record executive Scott Borchetta, a 20-year veteran of the music business, known for his work with Universal Records and for assisting Toby Keith in his rise to fame.

Struck by Taylor's performance, Scott approached the Swifts after the show. Taylor remembers the evening well. She knew the record executive had been concentrating on her music,

because he'd been listening with his eyes closed. "I have good news and I have bad news," he said to her. "The good news is that I want to sign you to a record deal. The bad news is that I'm no longer with Universal Records."

Scott was actually launching his own record label.

"He didn't have a name for it," Taylor recalled in a *CMT Insider* interview. "He didn't have a building for it. And he didn't have a staff for it. But he had a dream, and would I come on board? I went with my gut instinct which just said, 'Say yes.'"

Looking back, Taylor realized it was a risky choice. "There are a million ways it could've gone wrong," she noted.

It didn't go wrong. In fact, it went very right. Borchetta launched Big Machine Records in 2005 and the independent record label became a music sensation, also representing stars like Trisha Yearwood and Jack Ingram.

Taylor Swift—the little girl who turned her pain into music; the little girl who played guitar until her fingers bled—was now on the verge of making music history.

Chapter Two

A "Swift" Rise to Fame

That night at The Bluebird Café changed Taylor's life dramatically. At 15, she was still earning straight As at Hendersonville High School, but, after school, she wrote songs to jumpstart her music career with Big Machine Records. Attending both high school and songwriting sessions within the same day felt like a "double life" to Taylor.

"I walked around, talked to people, studied for tests, and had crushes on boys," Taylor told *Elle*. "And then after school, I would go downtown to Music Row in Nashville, and I would write songs about those experiences." Taylor soon met experienced songwriter Liz Rose, and the two began to collaborate on material. "My sessions with Taylor were some of the easiest I've ever done," Liz told *Blender* magazine. "Basically, I was just her editor. She'd write about what happened to her in school that day. She had such a clear vision of what she was trying to say. And she'd come in with some of the most incredible hooks."

First Hit Single

One day, in August 2005, Taylor came in with a song she'd written in math class about her ex-boyfriend, Drew, who had left to go away to college. It was about the pain of having to say good-bye at the end of summer and the memories that remained even though the relationship ended. The lyrics were both playful and sad and included the name of a well-known country star: "When you think Tim McGraw/I hope you think my favorite

song/The one we danced to all night long."

Taylor did not think the song would be a hit. "I completely forgot about it," she explained to *Florida Entertainment Scene*, "until I was playing my record label president (Scott Borchetta) a few songs, and my dad said 'Hey, play him that Tim McGraw song you wrote' and with some hesitation...I did."

Country is not a market for teen performers, and Scott Borchetta had taken a chance by signing the young Taylor Swift. But any doubts he might have had about Taylor's potential probably disappeared when he heard her sing, "Tim McGraw."

"Do you realize what you have just written?" he asked after hearing the song. "Do you have any idea?"

The song also impressed her writing partner, and Liz Rose worked with Taylor at the piano to make it even better. When it came time to select Taylor's first single, the choice was obvious. Big Machine Records released "Tim McGraw" in June 2006. It peaked at No. 6 on the Billboard Country Songs chart and at No. 40 on the Billboard Hot 100 chart.

In October, Taylor released her self-titled album, which included other top ten singles on the Country Songs chart: "Teardrops on My Guitar," "Our Song," "Should've Said No," and "Picture to Burn." The album worked its way up to No.1 on the Country Albums chart and No. 5 on the *Billboard* 200 chart. By June 2008, the album went platinum, which means it sold one million copies. It was a historic achievement. Taylor Swift was the first female solo country artist to write or co-write every song on a platinum album. The single "Our Song," which was No. 1 on the Country Songs chart for six weeks, also made history. Taylor was the youngest country singer to write and sing a number one song on that chart.

Taylor was at the Country Music Association (CMA) Music Fest in Nashville when she heard she went platinum. "It was the coolest thing to get told that sort of thing in front of fans, simply because they're the only reason why my album went platinum," said Taylor, who was signing autographs at the time. "It was such an awesome feeling, and some days I STILL can't believe it!"

It was a big win for Taylor, but also for Big Machine Records, the little record label that could. They were starting to get more recognition,

What Tim McGraw thinks of "Tim McGraw"

■ When Taylor Swift wrote the ballad "Tim McGraw," she had never met the handsome country superstar, the son of the late Tug McGraw, who played for both the New York Mets and the Philadelphia Phillies. Taylor said the song wasn't actually about Tim McGraw.

"The song is about two people who fall in love and are brought together by country music," she told the *Tennessean*. "And even when they're apart, every time they hear that song, it takes them right back to that place. For me, the song is about the haunting power of country music, one of the reasons I love it so much."

So, what did Tim McGraw think of the tune that bears his name?

"I love it," he said, after Taylor's agent played the song for him. "But I'm no George Jones. I'm not a legend or anything."

Taylor appreciated this modest response. "I thought that was really cool," she said, "because it was a really good indicator of why he's gotten where he is. He's still humble about his success."

At first, Tim wasn't sure if he should be flattered by the tribute or if he should feel old. "The more I hear it," he said. "...I start taking it as a compliment."

Almost a year after the song's release, the two country singers finally met on May 15, 2007, at the Academy of Country Music Awards. That night, Taylor, who was nominated for "Top New Female Artist," played a solo acoustic version of "Tim McGraw." Afterward, she met Tim McGraw on live television. "Hi, I'm Taylor," she said to him. By that point, they were both platinum-selling musicians.

Over time, Tim McGraw and his wife, the beautiful and talented country singer Faith Hill, befriended Taylor Swift. They send her presents on her birthday and even let her stay at their house when she visits Los Angeles.

In addition to giving impromptu concerts, Taylor also takes photos with her fans. Above, she posed with two of her most enthusiastic male admirers.

Airports and Ice-Cream Shops

■ It's no secret: Taylor Swift loves her fans. In fact, she's known for pulling out her guitar and singing an impromptu concert for a small group of admirers.

Once, at the Nashville International Airport, a few fans approached her and asked her to play a song. "So, I got my band members to bust out their guitars, too, and we just played a concert at the terminal," Taylor recalled to *Allure*. "It's so much fun doing stuff like that."

Another time, Taylor was taking a break from performing in Fresno, California, and went out for ice cream. The girl working the register recognized Taylor right away. She told the country star how she listened to Taylor's music when she cleaned up the shop at the end of the night. Of course, Taylor and two of her band members pulled out their instruments and put on a mini-concert.

"It was so great because the girl called all her family and friends and pretty soon we had quite the crowd in that Fresno ice cream shop," remembered Taylor. "I love being in situations where I can entertain people and play my music. For so long, all through high school, no one ever really understood my passion for music. I was always on the outside...so to know that people are now embracing me for my music, it is such an amazing feeling."

thanks to Taylor Swift.

"Being on a little record label, you have to fight harder than being on a bigger record label to be on award shows, to be a performer and a presenter, and to get big tours and support," Taylor told *Billboard* magazine. "My record label had 12 employees when I put out my album and my single, and I just kept looking around and thinking, 'Some day we are going to grow, and this is going to change, and we are going to have a fighting chance.'"

Big Machine Records did grow, especially when Taylor Swift's music crossed over into the pop genre.

Crossing Over

Usually, country music has its own specific set of fans, but some country artists "cross over" to other genres, like pop. LeAnn Rimes and Shania Twain both found pop appeal in the 1990s, and Taylor Swift did it in 2007 with "Teardrops on My Guitar," a song about a girl in love with a boy unaware of her feelings. The song first came out on country radio, but broke the music barrier after Taylor made what she called a "no-brainer" decision, a small change to the song. "We put a beat behind it and turned it into a song that they would play on pop radio," she said, according to MTV.com.

That little background beat brought Taylor to the Billboard Hot 100, where "Teardrops on My Guitar" peaked at No. 13. It later peaked at No. 5 on the Mediabase Top 40 and Billboard Adult Contemporary chart. "Teardrops on My Guitar" gained even more popularity when the music video played on MTV and VH1. It wasn't long before Taylor Swift

Taylor toured with Kenny Chesney in 2008; like Kenny—whose song "No Shoes, No Shirt, No Problems" was a crossover hit—Taylor crossed over into the pop genre.

became a name everybody—country and pop music fans—knew. More of her songs, including "Our Song," which she wrote for a ninth grade talent show, proved successful in the pop market.

Crossing over is something Taylor counts as a major success. "So many girls come up and say to me, 'I have never listened to country music in my life. I didn't even know my town had

a country music station. Then I got your record, and now I'm obsessed,'" she explained in a *Time* interview, based on questions from fans. "That's the coolest compliment to me."

It's a compliment, because, statistically, youth do not listen to country music. But thanks to Taylor Swift—and other contemporary country crossover stars like Carrie Underwood and Kellie Pickler—young

"There's heartache in her songs and her voice. It feels fresh, because the rawest heartbreak is probably the first heartbreak." —Scott Borchetta, President of Big Machine Records music fans are warming to the genre. It's a triumph Taylor said she did not plan. "I would go to CRS (Country Radio Seminar) before I was ever signed to a record deal, and I would listen to people say, 'Someone needs to bring in that younger demographic,'" she explained to *Entertainment Weekly*. "And what I'm hearing is that we've done that, and we kind of stumbled upon it. I wasn't trying to be exclusive as to who would like it."

One of the reasons Taylor draws so many fans, especially young ones, is her use of social networking sites like MySpace and Facebook. There, she updates her blogs, posts personal videos, and even responds to fans' comments. She also "tweets" regularly on Twitter. Her official website, TaylorSwift.com, boasts a scrapbook/diary format and is very fan-friendly. Dozens of fans have created their own websites to honor Taylor.

By the fall of 2009, Taylor had more than 1.5 million fans on MySpace and 2.3 million fans on Facebook. In March 2009, she hit the 200 million mark for music streams on MySpace.

Taylor said her success via the internet was an accident. "I created my MySpace page in eighth grade, because that's how all my friends talked to each other, so I made one too," she said, according to GACtv.com. "Then, all of a sudden, my friends started putting my songs on their profiles, and then their relatives and their friends in different states did. And by the time I went to my first radio interview, I already had this grassroots following."

In addition to being an Internet sensation, Taylor also maintains a large number of middle-aged female fans, whom the music industry claimed

only wanted to hear male singers. Her songs, like "Tim McGraw" and "Teardrops on My Guitar" may be about young love, but they have a universal appeal, said Scott Borchetta, who noted her fans range in age from eight to 38.

"She's a teen, but there's no bubblegum aspect to it," he noted. "There's heartache in her songs and her voice. It feels fresh, because the rawest heartbreak is probably the first heartbreak. Some people connect with Taylor's songs because they're right in that moment, and some because they're nostalgic about it."

Even Jay Frank, senior vice president of Country Music Television (CMT), recognized Taylor's successful crossover. "She's become a much bigger artist than the country format," he said.

On the Road

Taylor began touring with other country music stars at the onset of her career. Her self-titled album was out only a month when she opened for Rascal Flatts, a country band known for their crossover hit "What Hurts the Most" and a remake of Tom Cochrane's "Life is a Highway," featured on the Disney Pixar *Cars* soundtrack. She toured with Rascal Flatts again in 2007.

In January 2007, the legendary country artist George Strait invited Taylor Swift to serve as his opening act for that year's arena tour. Taylor was thrilled. "Just last week I was at the CMA Awards watching him be inducted into the Hall of Fame," she said. "This is surreal! I keep pinching myself to make sure this isn't just a dream."

Taylor's dream would continue throughout the year, as she joined country star Brad Paisley on his *Bonfires & Amplifiers Tour*, which included other music sensations like fellow Big Machine Records artist Jack Ingram and Kellie Pickler of *American Idol*.

"I was looking at a lot of artists to come out on tour with us, but as soon as I downloaded her album, I knew we had to have her," Brad told *Blender* magazine. "I was floored by the songwriting. I love the fact that she doesn't pretend to be 30 years old in her songs. She has a very genuine voice."

Taylor had fun touring with Brad Paisley. She and the other performers even played a prank on him during his performance of a single called "Ticks."

"I went online, and I ordered these giant tick costumes—like big, giant sumo-wrestler-looking tick costumes—and me and Kellie (Pickler) dressed up in them and ran out on stage and started dancing all around him," ex-

plained Taylor, who posted a video of the prank on her MySpace page. "And then Jack Ingram, the other opening act, came out in this white exterminator suit halfway through the song, with a sprayer, and proceeded to kill us onstage."

In the summer of 2007, Taylor also opened for the man who helped jumpstart her career: Tim McGraw. She joined Tim and Faith Hill on their Soul2Soul Tour, along with Lori McKenna and The Warren Brothers. During the last show, the couple showered her with a beautiful flower bouquet. In early 2008, Taylor also toured with Kenny Chesney in his *Keg in the Closet* tour.

While serving as an opening act at these venues, Taylor Swift learned the ropes from some of country music's finest performers, experiences she would later use on her own headlining tour, *Fearless*. On the road, she enjoyed seeing how each performer handled the tour differently.

"Kenny is up at the crack of dawn, walking around the venue, getting to know everyone, from the sound-check guys to the people who sell the souvenirs to the fans," she told *USA*

Weekend. "Then, Rascal Flatts stages this big production with all the flash. And George Strait? It's all about the music with him. He pays so much attention to building up the song, with the arrangements and the band and his singing."

And the Award Goes to...

It wasn't long before the music industry officially recognized Taylor for her talent. In April 2007, Taylor won "Breakthrough Video of the Year" for "Tim McGraw" at the CMT Music Awards, where the winners are chosen by fan votes. Taylor took her mom as her date that night, but she made a point to thank her fans.

"This is for my MySpace people and everybody who voted," said Taylor, who treated the evening like prom night, because she didn't attend the formal dance at school. "The fans, y'all, I'm going out on tour with Brad Paisley and this is coming with me to every single [autograph] signing line, so you can get a picture of the award you won for me."

Taylor made good on her promise; the award actually came with her to signings. She went on to receive more honors that year, but not all of them were awards. For starters, she was asked to perform at the "CMA Music Festival: Country's Night to Rock," which aired in July 2007 on ABC. To Taylor, the invite was a form of recognition.

"It was such an amazing feeling, because I have always considered that show to be a huge moment for any artist's career," she said. "Like a really good sign that you're doing the right things, and you're on your way. I freaked out, as usual, and started screaming."

Superstar of Tomorrow

■ Taylor's award-show honors are almost too many to count. Below is a list of other awards she has either been nominated for or won.

Teen's Choice:
In 2008, Taylor won "Breakout Artist of the Year." In 2009, she was nominated for "Love Song" and "Music Tour," but won for "Female Artist" and "Female Album."

People's Choice:
In 2009, Taylor's "Love Story" was nominated for "Favorite Country Song."

Young Hollywood Awards:
In 2008, Taylor won "Superstar of Tomorrow."

CMT Online Awards:
Many of Taylor's songs were nominated for this fan-voted award, but in 2007, "Teardrops on My Guitar" won for No. 1 Streamed Studio 330 Sessions Video.

Taylor has also won awards, or been nominated for them, in Australia, Canada, and Thailand.

That October, after she released *Sounds of the Season: The Taylor Swift Holiday Collection*, she won the Nashville Songwriters Association International's 2007 Songwriter/Artist of the Year, an honor she shared with country music veteran Alan Jackson. Because the prestigious award—granted to artists such as Garth Brooks and Shania Twain in past years—is voted on by peers, other professional songwriters, Taylor took it to heart.

"I don't even know how to explain how honored I feel," she said, according to GACtv.com. "I mean, I was sitting at the table and they called Alan Jackson's name and I'm just like, 'Oh my God! That's awesome!' And then all of the sudden, they say my name, and I'm like, 'What happened?' I'm so humbled by this experience. It's just so unbelievable."

Another big win came in November 2007, when she took home a BMI Country Award for co-writing the song "Tim McGraw." The next night, after Taylor performed "Our Song" during the CMA awards, she won the CMA's Horizon Award, a highly desirable prize that recognizes a country singer for performance, as well as creative growth and professionalism.

Taylor, just 17 at the time, gave a very enthusiastic acceptance speech at the CMAs. "This is definitely the highlight of my senior year!" she said, making the crowd—especially her parents—roar with laughter. After the show, Taylor restated how much the award meant to her.

"This was like a fairytale to me," she said. "I didn't know I could be this happy! I didn't think I would ever experience a night so magical in my life!" She thanked her record label and many people behind-the-scenes, like her band, crew, and even the bus drivers "who have sacrificed time with their families this year, so that I could live my dream."

In December 2007, Taylor rounded out the year with a Grammy nomination for Best New Artist. Because she was presenting Grammy nominations that day with Fergie of the Black Eyed Peas and R & B singer Akon, she was on stage when her name was announced. When she heard her name, she brought a hand to her mouth and proceeded to hug a number of people on stage: Fergie, comedian George Lopez, and Taylor Hawkins and Dave Grohl of the Foo Fighters.

In that category, Taylor was up against some big names: Amy Winehouse, Feist, Ledisi and Paramore. "It's an all-genre nomination," she said of the nomination. "So it's everybody — rock, pop, hip-hop — so the fact that I was included is awesome."

When February rolled around, Taylor attended the Grammys with an "it's great just to be nominated" attitude, thanks to some advice from her mother. "My mom sat me down and said, 'You need to have a good night whether you win or not,'" Taylor told the *Reading Eagle*.

In the end, Amy Winehouse nabbed the award, but it was an experience Taylor would not soon forget. Besides, Taylor had another honor to smile about. She was the best-selling artist of all genres in 2008.

Triple Platinum

In April 2008, Taylor Swift's self-titled album went triple platinum, meaning three million copies were sold. She announced the news on *Good Morning America*, where she had appeared in 2006 on the day she released the self-titled album.

"It's freaking me out," Taylor told co-host Robin Roberts of going multi-platinum "I'm so excited."

In kind, Robin Roberts told Taylor, "The world is discovering you now. You are considered *the* up and coming."

Her statement could not have been truer. That same month, Taylor won "Video of the Year" and "Female Video of the Year" for "Our Song" at the CMT Music Awards. In May 2008, Taylor finally took home "Top New Female Vocalist" at the ACM Awards; she'd been nominated the year prior, but lost to Carrie Underwood.

At the ACM Awards, Taylor performed the song "Should've Said No" about a cheating boyfriend under a cascading waterfall. She mentioned the stage stunt on her MySpace blog. "I've dreamt about that performance since I was in middle school," she wrote. "I've always wanted to perform an angry song and have water rain down from the ceiling and have a little freak-out onstage."

Her wet performance caught the attention of some pretty big stars that night. "People have asked me why I looked so surprised at the end," Taylor said. "Because I saw George Strait giving me a standing ovation."

The fall of 2008 would prove even more thrilling for Taylor, as far as awards and performances go. In October, she sang the National Anthem in Philadelphia for the World Series, which the Phillies won. It was a surreal experience for Taylor because she sang "The Star-Spangled Banner" for the minor league team, The Reading Phillies, when she was just ten years old.

In November, "Teardrops on my Guitar" was named "Country Song of the Year" at the BMI Country Awards. "Our Song" was also recognized as a winning song there. Later that month, Taylor was named "Favorite Female Country Artist" at the American Music Awards (AMA), the rival award show to the Grammys.

continued on page 34

The Homeschool Decision

■ Taylor attended Hendersonville High School for her freshman and sophomore years. There, she met best friend Abigail Anderson, performed in the talent show, and dated a few boys who would later make it into the lyrics of her songs. Once her career took off, however, she had to make a difficult decision about her education. It would be hard to balance her high school schedule with tours and performances. Therefore, she left Hendersonville High School to enter a homeschool program with Aaron Academy, a private Christian school.

"My brother's always calling me the dropout of the family," Taylor joked.

It was a decision Taylor felt was necessary to further her career, and thus far, she doesn't regret it, though she sometimes considers how her life may have been different if she'd stayed in high school. "You're always going to wonder about the road not taken, the dorm not taken and the sorority not taken," she explained. "But if I wasn't doing this, I would've missed out on the best moments I've ever known and the most wonderful life that I still can't believe I get to live."

Due to an excellent homeschool curriculum, Taylor was able to graduate in the summer of 2008, the same time she would have graduated if she'd attended Hendersonville High School all four years. Now that she has her diploma, is college next for Taylor Swift?

"I always thought that I would go to college, most definitely," said Taylor. "But then I really thought about it and assessed the situation, and I can't leave this life. Going to college would mean saying good-bye to my music career, and I just can't do that."

Taylor's brother, Austin, who attended Pope John Paul II High School in Hendersonville, is always calling Taylor the "dropout of the family."

"I love the whole crime scene aspect of it," Taylor said of the television show CSI. *"Figuring things out and analyzing."*

Live from New York, It's Taylor Swift!

■ Due to the television broadcast of awards shows like the Grammys and CMAs and her music videos, Taylor Swift has enjoyed many moments singing on TV. She also appeared in an episode of CMT's "Crossroads" with Def Leppard, a rock band she and her mom both love.

She was granted the opportunity to show off her acting skills as well. In January 2009, she was the youngest country musical guest to appear on *SNL*. In addition to performing two songs as musical guest, she played a small role as the red-haired Little Orphan Annie. In a skit about the downfall of Broadway shows, she sang the "The Sun Will Come Out Tomorrow" before turning into a tough, street version of Annie. The performance was especially important for Taylor; it took place on her mom's birthday.

Later that same year, in March, Taylor also appeared on an episode of one of her favorite shows, *CSI*. "My dream is to die

on *CSI*," she often joked with her family and friends. "I've always wanted to be like one of the characters on there that they're trying to figure out what happened to."

Taylor especially likes *CSI: Las Vegas* for its video editing. "I love the whole crime scene aspect of it," she said of her

Taylor posed with Jamie Foxx and Corinne Foxx backstage during the 44th annual Academy of Country Music Awards. She also co-starred with the Ray actor in the Gary Marshall film, Valentine's Day.

obsession with crime shows. "Figuring things out and analyzing."

On the show, Taylor played Haley, a rebellious teen who is murdered at a motel run by her parents. Taylor's performance drew 21 million viewers.

After *CSI*, Taylor appeared on an episode of the game show *Opportunity Knocks*, as well as

MTV's House of Style. She's also run the talk show circuit, appearing on *The Ellen DeGeneres Show*, *The Late Show with David Letterman*, *Oprah*, and *The Tonight Show*, to name a few.

She's even made her way to the big screen. In *Hannah Montana: The Movie*, released in April 2009, she made a cameo performance.

During a scene at a country music fundraiser, Taylor gets up on stage to sing the romantic ballad "Crazier," which appears on the movie's soundtrack.

In February 2010, Taylor will make her onscreen acting debut, with a minor role in *Valentine's Day*, a Gary Marshall comedy about five interconnected love stories. Taylor acted opposite teen heartthrob Taylor Lautner of *Twilight*. The two play a prom king and queen and even share a kissing scene. The movie boasts a star-studded cast, including Jessica Alba, Jessica Biel, Patrick Dempsey, Jamie Foxx, Jennifer Garner, Anne Hathaway, Ashton Kutcher, and Julia Roberts.

What Happened After the VMAs

■ Immediately after the VMAs, Taylor answered questions backstage about Kanye West's interruption of her speech. "I was excited to be on-stage because I just won the award. And then I was excited that Kanye West was onstage," she said. "Then, I wasn't excited anymore."

She remained rather speechless about the evening, calling it "an interesting night." She did, however, open up more on *The View* two days later. "My overall thought process went something like, 'Wow, I can't believe I won, this is awesome, don't trip and fall, I'm going to get to thank the fans, this is so cool, oh, Kanye West is here, cool haircut, what are you doing here?'" Taylor told the ladies from *The View*. "And then, 'Ouch,' and then, 'I guess I'm not going to get to thank the fans.'"

At that point in time, Kanye had yet to apologize officially to Taylor for the incident. He had posted a message in all capital letters on his blog that said, "I'm sooooo sorry to Taylor Swift and her fans and her mom. I spoke to her mother right after and she said the same thing my mother would've said. She is very talented! ... I'm in the wrong for going on stage and taking away from her moment."

After Taylor's *View* appearance, Kanye called the 19-year-old to apologize formally. She accepted his apology and said he sounded sincere. Despite this truce, the Internet still buzzed with the story and clips of the shocking moment at the VMAs. Many e-mails and websites spoofed the Kanye mishap; they showed him interrupting the speeches of President Barack Obama and Yoda from *Star Wars*.

Some good things came of the incident, though. Taylor received flowers from Janet Jackson along with "the nicest card ever," and she was showered with support by friends, family, and fans. "Just everybody being supportive and showing love, it was really nice [to know] people I didn't even think knew who I was were out there having my back and being really very kind to me," Taylor said.

The story began to take its toll on Taylor, however. She answered many questions about the Kanye incident, but during one interview with a Florida DJ, she asked politely to move on to another topic. When the DJ did not back down, she actually stopped doing the interview and moved on to another one.

continued from page 30

Despite these honors, the biggest news in November 2008 was the release of Taylor's much anticipated sophomore album, *Fearless*.

Fearless

"It's a big deal to title your album, so I wanted to make sure that is was the right call," Taylor said of the 13-song album. "I started thinking about the word 'fearless' and what it means to me. It isn't that you're completely unafraid. I think fearless is having fears, but jumping anyway."

Taylor took a big jump with Fearless, right onto The Billboard 200. It debuted at No. 1 there and on the Country Albums chart. According to Nielsen SoundScan, 592,000 copies of the album were sold in the United States within the very first week. Digital copies totaled 129,000 in that first week. The album received rave reviews from music critics. Both The *Associated Press* and *The New York Times* named *Fearless* one of the top ten albums of the year. *Rolling Stone* named it one of the top 50 albums of the year.

Many of the singles from *Fearless* were already hits before the album was officially released. That's in part due to heavy radio play, and Taylor's early performances of songs. The first single "Love Story"—a happy-ending version of Shakespeare's Romeo & Juliet—was released in September 2008 and was on the Billboard 100 Top Ten by the following month. It went on to peak at No. 1 on the Top 40 radio chart (Mediabase), making Taylor the first country artist to do so.

The song "White Horse," about a fairytale romance that doesn't come true, appeared in a September 2008 episode of *Grey's Anatomy*, one of

Taylor's favorite television programs. "You should've seen tears streaming down my face when I got the phone call that they were going to use that song," Taylor told *Billboard* magazine. "I have never been that excited. This is my life's goal, to have a song on *Grey's Anatomy*. My love of *Grey's Anatomy* has never waivered. It's my longest relationship to date."

She also performed "White Horse" live for the first time at the American Music Awards in November 2008. She then performed "Love Story" again at the CMA awards in November, as well as on *Dick Clark's Rockin' New Year's Eve* show.

"I was blown away by how many people were there and how much confetti was coming down on us," said Taylor, who enjoyed her first time in Times Square that night with hosts Dick Clark and Ryan Seacrest. "I actually got a kiss on the cheek from Lionel Ritchie on New Year's Eve. So that's a pretty memorable experience."

In January 2009, she performed "Love Story" and "Forever and Always"—a feisty tune about ex-boyfriend Joe Jonas—on *Saturday Night Live (SNL)* hosted by Neil Patrick Harris of *How I Met Your Mother*.

The following month, she sang the then unreleased single "Fifteen"—about the trials and tribulations of high school life as seen through the eyes of a fifteen-year-old—at the Grammy awards with her good friend and fellow country/pop artist Miley Cyrus of *Hannah Montana*.

Other hit singles from the Fearless album included the crossover hit, "You Belong with Me;" "Fearless;" "Breathe," (which Taylor co-wrote with pop artist Colbie Caillat, who

also sings back-up vocals); and, "Change," which was chosen for the 2008 Olympic Games soundtrack.

After opening for stars like Tim McGraw, Faith Hill, and Brad Paisley, it was about time for Taylor to headline her own tour. On January 30, 2009, she announced her *Fearless Tour*, which started in April 2009 in Indiana and took her to Los Angeles, Chicago, and to the UK in November. (For more detailed coverage of Taylor's *Fearless Tour*, see Chapter 8).

A Bittersweet Moment

Fearless brought Taylor more success in regards to awards. In April 2009, it won "Album of the Year" at the 2009 ACM Awards, where Taylor also took home the Crystal Milestone Award. In June 2009, she won "Video of the Year" and "Female Video of the Year" for "Love Story" at the CMT Music Awards. There, she also broke out of her usual musical style to perform "Thug Story" with rapper T-Pain.

Oddly, while Taylor was receiving awards for songs from her *Fearless* album, she was still winning awards for songs from her first album as well. In May 2009, "Teardrops on My Guitar," from her self-titled album, won her a BMI Pop Award; that night, she also received the BMI President's Award, which is not an annual award, but one given when the industry wants to recognize an "exceptional person in the entertainment industry."

Taylor can act a bit 'fearless' on stage; she jammed with Rick "Sav" Savage of Def Leppard.

"Yo, Taylor, I...I'm really happy for you; I'm gonna let you finish. But Beyonce had one of the best videos of all time. One of the best videos of all time."
—Kanye West

Rapper Kanye West interrupted Taylor's acceptance speech at the 2009 MTV Video Music Awards.

pajamas and videotaped her reaction, which she then posted on her Mypace page. (See the Chapter 8 sidebar, Pajama Party).

But just a few days later, Taylor experienced a much publicized, bittersweet moment at the MTV Video Music Awards. In 2008, Taylor had been nominated for "Best New Artist" at the VMAs. The next year, she was up for "Best Female Video" for "You Belong with Me" against superstars like Beyonce Knowles. Despite the tough competition, Taylor made history once again that night by being the first country artist to win a Video Music Award. After mouthing "Oh my gosh," Taylor headed to the stage to accept her award.

"Thank you so much," she told the roaring crowd. "I always dreamed about what it would be like to maybe win one of these someday, but I never actually thought that it would happen. I sing country music, so thank you so much for giving me a chance to win a VMA award."

That was the extent of her speech, however, because rapper Kanye West stormed the stage and took control of the microphone. "Yo, Taylor, I...I'm really happy for you; I'm gonna let you finish," he told the confused and surprised 19-year-old. "But Beyonce had one of the best videos of all time. One of the best videos of all time."

Kanye was referring to Beyonce's video for "Single Ladies (Put a Ring on It)".

The crowd booed and a close-up shot of Beyonce revealed her mouthing the words "Oh my God." She looked as surprised as Taylor, but also dismayed. After Kanye left the stage, a few people in the audience stood and applauded a shaken-up

Both of her albums did well simultaneously. Her self-titled album reached the 4.2 million copies mark by June 2009, while Fearless went triple platinum that July and later hit the four million mark by late September.

September 2009 was a big month for Taylor, in good ways and bad. Taylor made history again when "You Belong with Me" climbed to No. 1 on the Mediabase Top 40 radio chart and

the Billboard Radio Songs chart. She was the first country singer to have two No. 1 songs there; "Love Story" was her first.

Earlier that month, she also received four nominations for the CMAs: "Music Video of the Year," "Album of the Year," "Female Vocalist of the Year," and "Entertainer of the Year." Taylor watched the announcements of the nominees in her

Taylor to finish her speech.

"I would like to thank the fans and MTV. Thank you," was all Taylor said before leaving the stage with her award. Later in the show, when Beyonce won for "Video of the Year", she gave Taylor a second chance to give her acceptance speech.

"I remember being 17-years-old, up for my first MTV award with Destiny's Child, and it was one of the most exciting moments in my life," Beyonce said. "So I would like for Taylor to come out and have her moment."

Taylor Swift then returned from backstage to a cheering crowd and, after hugging Beyonce, said, "Maybe we could try this again."

With the microphone safely in her possession, she went on to thank the director of the video, as well as the actors, and, most of all, her fans on MySpace and Twitter.

Dealing with Fame

After the VMAs, Taylor Swift experienced the downside of being famous. She wanted to forget what happened and move on, but the story was everywhere on the Internet, newsstands and television.

Of course, media attention is part of the job. Stars often lose their privacy, and Taylor is no exception. Once, while shopping at Victoria's Secret, she realized a group of people were watching her. "I look up and there are, like, 15 people looking at me, with camera phones out, waiting to take a picture of which kind of underwear I'm going to buy," she explained to *Women's Health*. "'*Think she's a small or an extra small?*' I wanted to be, like, 'Uh, guys? I can hear you.'"

Despite this invasion of privacy, Taylor said she doesn't mind public-

Taylor posed for a quick photo with a fan.

ity. "I am never going to be that 'Get out of my face' girl," she said. Fortunately, Taylor is able to live a fairly normal life when she returns home to Tennessee. She lives in Nashville, not Hollywood, so that helps. The paparazzi are not as visible there, although that trend is slowly changing.

Taylor has become so big, she's even moved into the world of merchandising. In 2008, in between her first and second album releases, she put out the Wal-Mart exclusive "Beautiful Eyes" a six-song CD of old and new songs that included a behind-the-scenes DVD as well. She also started her own line of L.E.I sundresses at Wal-Mart, and Jakks Pacific put out a doll in her likeness, complete with a ball gown and guitar.

All things considered, Taylor would never trade in her success. It's something she has dreamed about since she was a little girl. At age 13, she began writing in a journal everyday—there are 25 total, locked up in a safe at home—

and now that she's older, she looks back on those writings and can't believe how her dreams have come true.

"It's crazy to go back and read them, and think about all these things I once thought were so out of reach. I made this goal sheet when I was like 14 or 15 and it was like 'My life will be complete if...I win a CMA award, have a platinum record, have a number one song,'" she told *Seventeen* magazine while being interviewed for a cover story. "And I swear to you, one of the goals was to be on the cover of Seventeen magazine. So I am checking these things off the list, and I'm like, 'You're kidding me!'"

Taylor may have dreamed of being a star, but she's still shocked by her success and fame.

"Not in a million years did I ever think this would work out," she told *Self*. "What blows me away the most is that anyone actually cares what I have to say."

Chapter Three

Secrets of Success

In only a few years time, Taylor Swift—once an unknown, 11-year-old trying to get a record deal on Music Row—became a country and pop music superstar. Her instant fame raises an important question: What's the secret of Taylor's success?

"I think the first thing you should know is that nobody in country music 'made it' the same way," Taylor told *CMT News*. "It's all different. There's no blueprint for success, and sometimes you just have to work at it. You should make sure that you know who you are as an artist and make sure it's nothing like everyone else. It's good to be inspired by other artists, but you should always make sure that you've got your own niche."

Taylor certainly has a niche. It's no secret Taylor Swift is beautiful. Slender and tall—she's 5'11" and over 6' in heels—she resembles a runway model. Both male and female fans adore her curly blonde hair and piercing blue eyes. But her fans equally appreciate who she is on the *inside*. Her music and storytelling captures their hearts.

Taylor is a true musician; she plays guitar and writes her own songs. Songwriting has always been at the forefront of her career. It's one of the reasons she walked away from RCA Records; they would not promise her songwriting privileges. "I didn't want to just be another girl singer," Taylor said. "I wanted there to be something that set me apart. And I knew that had to be my writing."

Her songwriting does set her apart, even from other songwriters, because her songs are based on personal experience. She writes the kind of songs she liked to listen to when she was a kid. Back then, she would fall in love with a song and wonder whom the tune had been written about. "It would have totally broken my heart to know it wasn't about anyone, and was just written so it could be on the radio," she explained to *Seventeen*.

The Name Game

Taylor Swift's songs are so personal and descriptive, they are a true extension of her journal or diary. She even works the real names of ex-crushes and ex-boyfriends right into the lyrics.

"I have no issue with naming names," she told *Rolling Stone*. "I think that it's sort of fun for me to know that when the album comes out, there are going to be people who are going hear about it. My personal goal for my songs is to be so detailed that the guy the song is written about knows it's about him."

This honesty in songwriting is part of her appeal. Fans young and old enjoy the "tell-all" feel of her songs. Taylor writes and sings about some distressing topics: cheating boyfriends, bad break-ups, unrequited love and the high school popularity contest, to name a few. She reveals her personal heartbreaks and insecurities through her music.

"I think it's better to be real than to be protected all the time," she told *Self*. "Everybody's vulnerable; it's just how much you choose to show it."

She compared her songwriting—which she said helps her "vent"—to an art or a hobby. "For some people, they like to paint. Others like to shop and buy the cutest pair of shoes, and that's the art they get to wear on their feet," she said. "For me, it's writing."

In this way, songwriting helps her process her emotions. It allows her to make sense of her feelings or the end of a relationship. "It's my way of coping," she told *Women's Health*. "I write when I'm frustrated, angry, or confused. I've figured out a way to filter all of that into something good."

Teen Life

Taylor's success is partly due to her ability to connect with her fans' experiences. She understands pre-teen and teen issues because she was the same age, going through the exact same things, when she wrote her songs.

"She very much lives in her demographic," Big Machine Records president Scott Borchetta said. "I can ask her, 'Is this something your fans will like?' and she has a great innate sense about what people her age are into and what they're not."

Trying to fit in with the "cool crowd" at school is one of the issues Taylor tackles in songwriting. "The Outside," which originally appeared on Maybelline's *Chicks with Attitude* CD and later on her self-titled album, was based on Taylor's own experiences in junior high, where she was "dumped" by a cool clique of girls. Taylor wrote the song when she was 12 years old, and the lyrics reveal the pain she felt as an outcast: "How can I ever try to be better/Nobody ever lets me in/I can still see you, this ain't the best view/On the outside looking in."

"I wrote that about the scariest feeling I've ever felt: going to school, walking down the hall, looking at all those faces, and not knowing who you're gonna talk to that day," Taylor explained. "People always ask, 'How did you have the courage to walk up to record labels when you were 12 or 13?' It's because I could never feel the kind of rejection in the music industry that I felt in middle school."

"It's my way of coping," she told Women's Health. *"I write when I'm frustrated, angry, or confused. I've figured out a way to filter all of that into something good."*

"I can't stop writing. I can't turn it off. I go through situations, and I go through experiences, and I go through life, and I need to write it.... It's like breathing."

Another song, "Tied Together With a Smile," deals with body image. Taylor said she wrote the song about one of her friends, an attractive, popular girl. "Every guy wanted to be with her, every girl wanted to be her," Taylor said of this friend. "I wrote that song the day I found out she had an eating disorder."

The girl confessed to Taylor that she was bulimic, which means she would eat as much food as she wanted but make herself throw up to stay thin. It was hard to believe because the girl seemed so perfect. "But sometimes when you get a little closer to people who look that perfect, you realize that they don't *feel* perfect," Taylor explained to *Seventeen*. "They feel like they're ugly."

It was difficult news for Taylor to hear. She didn't want to make the girl feel even worse about herself. Taylor likes to reason with people and always stay calm. "After awhile, I was just like 'You don't need to do that anymore,'" she said. "So I played that song ("Tied Together with a Smile") for her and I said, 'Who do you think it's about?' And honestly, I don't think she ever did it after that."

Taylor doesn't specifically mention bulimia in the song, but she describes a teenage girl who feels bad about the way she looks. "Seems the only one who doesn't see your beauty/Is the face in the mirror looking back at you," the lyrics state. "You walk around here thinking you're not pretty/But that's not true, 'cause I know you."

According to Taylor, the most personal song she's ever written is "Fifteen" from her *Fearless* album. At age 15, many teens are starting high school and beginning to figure out who they are and who they want to be. "My best friend (Abigail Anderson) and I met our freshman year of high school and our lives absolutely changed," said Taylor about the song. "I walked away from love, and then I

Q & A: Taylor's Writing Process

How long does it take Taylor to write a song?
"Most of the time, songs that I write end up being finished in 30 minutes or less," Taylor told *Time*. "'Love Story' I wrote on my bedroom floor in about 20 minutes. When I get on a roll with something, it's really hard for me to put it down unfinished."

When is Taylor most inspired to write?
"I usually get inspired to write in the middle of the night," she told *Country Weekly*. "I'll come up with an amazing idea, and I'll think, 'Oh . . . I'll remember it the next morning.' Then you never remember it the next morning! So I've always gotta have some sort of recording device near me when I'm sleeping."

What happens when Taylor tries to write a song but nothing comes to mind?
"That happens all the time," Taylor told *CMT News*. "What I do is just put the guitar down and wait for something to hit me. You can never push songwriting. It happens or it doesn't."

What's more important, the words or the music?
"I love lyrics more than notes," she admitted. "A song is a favorite song not because the singer can hit and hold a high note but because of the words, their meaning."

How many songs has Taylor written?
"It's got to be about 500. I absolutely can't stop writing songs," she told *Rolling Stone*. "It's funny because sometimes you'll hear artists talking about how they have to hurry up and write this next record and it's like, I can't stop writing. I can't turn it off. I go through situations, and I go through experiences, and I go through life, and I need to write it…. It's like breathing."

What's Taylor's best advice for aspiring songwriters?
"Write your songs not for a demographic or for getting on the radio," she told *Time*. "Write your songs for the person you're writing that song about. When I sit down, I say to myself, 'OK, who is this about? What would I say to him right now if I could?'"

walked into a record label. I walked onto a tour, and that is how my story ended. Abigail, my best friend, got her heart ripped out, and I was there and went through it with her, but I am really glad that I was able to write it down."

"Fifteen" is a song that appeals to fans of all ages. It's a reflective tune, looking back on a time when most people don't know what's truly important in life. Middle-age listeners appreciate the song's positive message: "But in your life you'll do things greater than dating the boy on the football team/I didn't know it at fifteen."

Young Love

Adolescence is also the time when people first experience romantic love. Taylor is no exception, and she's written many songs about romance. Her first hit single "Tim McGraw" was about the end of a summer relationship, one she would remember fondly whenever a Tim McGraw song played on the radio.

"I'm fascinated by love rather than the principle of 'Oh, does this guy like me?'" she said. "I love love. I love studying it and watching it. I love thinking about how we treat each other, and the crazy way that one person can feel one thing and another can feel totally different."

"Our Song," which Taylor wrote for the ninth grade talent show at Hendersonville High School, explores a fun side of relationships. Many couples claim a favorite song, a tune that represents the love they share. But what if a couple doesn't have a song? Could their song be some-thing else, like a sound? In "Our Song" Taylor sings: "Our song is a slamming screen door, sneakin' out late, tapping on your window."

"When I wrote that song, I was dating this guy who was going to be there at the talent show," Taylor told *The Reading Eagle*. "And we didn't have a song. I thought I'd just sing it in front of everyone at the high school. He was my first boyfriend, and no one at the school had heard me sing ever. It helped me fit in, I guess."

Taylor's song "Fearless," the first track on the album of the same name, explores another aspect of young love: the first date. It's about the exhilaration you feel at the beginning of a relationship when anything is possible. "It is about an incredible first date when all your walls are coming down," Taylor told *Cosmo Girl*. "And you are fearlessly jumping into love."

Another romantic song, "Love Story," retells the tale of *Romeo & Juliet*, with a twist. Unlike Shakespeare's tragic play, the song ends happily with a marriage proposal. Taylor wrote the song after she almost dated a boy her parents and friends did not like. "I spun it in the direction of *Romeo & Juliet*—our parents are fighting," explained Taylor. "I relate to it more as a love that you cannot really elaborate on, a love that maybe society wouldn't accept, a love that maybe your friends wouldn't accept."

Taylor believes "Love Story" is her most romantic song, even though it's about someone she didn't actually date. The song proves she's a

How to Decode Taylor's Lyrics

■ There's more to a Taylor Swift song than what meets the ears. A closer look at the lyrics printed inside the CD jackets of both *Fearless* and her self-titled album reveal secret messages. Taylor got the idea from The Beatles.

"They used to play around with secret messages in their records," Taylor told *USA Today*. "I figured you can't play a CD backward, but with encoding stuff into the lyrics, I was able to get a similar kind of thing across."

Want to decode Taylor's lyrics? It's easy. Find the random capital letters within a song and write them down in the order they appear. Each song spells out a unique phrase.

good storyteller; she can spin beautiful tales about relationships she didn't even have. That happens a lot, because Taylor is often inspired by other people's life experiences. In fact, the idea for "You Belong with Me" came to her through eavesdropping. One day, Taylor was on her band's bus and overheard a phone conversation between one of her band members and his girlfriend. "The guy was going 'Baby, of course I love you more than music. I'm so sorry. I had to go to sound check. I'm so sorry I didn't stay on the phone with you,'" Taylor explained to *Self*. "And immediately in my head, I get this line: 'You're on the phone with your girlfriend, she's upset; she's going off about something that you said.' And it all came to me at once. I bolted to my bus. I elaborated the story and related it to another situation because I don't have a crush on a member of my band. But I do know what it's like to want someone who's got someone who takes him for granted."

Apparently, her fans know what it's like too, because "You Belong with Me" became a No. 1 crossover hit.

Heartbreak

With every love comes the possibility of heartbreak, and Taylor has experienced her share of those. She writes about the negative side of love as well as the positive.

"I think I'm very fascinated by the differences between reality and fairy tales. When we're little, we read these books and we see cartoons and the bad guy is always wearing black. You always know who he is," she said. "But in real life, the bad guy can be incredibly charming and have a great smile and perfect hair. He says

things that make you laugh, and he's sweet and he's funny, but you don't realize he's going to cause you a lot of pain." The song "White Horse" off her *Fearless* album describes this

difference between a real romance and the fairy tale version often seen in movies. "I'm not a princess/This ain't a fairytale/I'm not the one you'll sweep of her feet/Lead her up the stairwell," Taylor wrote with Liz Rose. "This ain't Hollywood/This is a small town/ I was a dreamer before you went and let me down/ Now it's too late for you and your white horse to come around."

Taylor is very proud of "White

Horse," largely because of the music. The song boasts guitar, piano and cello. But she's also proud of the lyrics, which describe the moment you realize a relationship is not going to

work out. "That moment is the most earth-shattering moment," she told *Billboard*.

Taylor's other heartbreak songs take on more than a fairytale gone wrong. "Should've Said No" is about a cheating boyfriend, "Picture to Burn" is about a guy who didn't like Taylor in return, and "Forever and Always" is about promises not kept. (See Chapter Four for the true boyfriend stories that inspired these tunes).

No Regrets

■ Taylor has revealed so much of herself in her songs, even the names of the boys who broke her heart. Does she ever regret being so honest?

"I don't think honesty is ever something you should regret," she said. "I figure if I'm going to cover things up and try to hide the way I feel and try to be perfect all the time, people are going to see through that."

Taylor writes songs about real people because "it is the only way I know how to do things. I can't wish I hadn't written a song about someone because if I hadn't, that song wouldn't exist," she told *Seventeen*.

There is one down side to naming names. Many people in her hometown of Hendersonville think Taylor has written a song about them. "You go out into this big world and you go on tour with all these people, and you go back and it's still a small town and they still gossip about it," Taylor told *Entertainment Weekly*. "I think it's one of everybody's favorite things to talk about—who my songs are written about. There are definitely a few more people who think that I've written songs about them than there actually are."

In her songs, Taylor may be speaking of teenage romances, but heartbreak is something people of all ages experience. "The drama and the trauma of the relationship you have when you're 16 can mirror the one you have when you're 26," Taylor told *Women's Health* "Life repeats itself."

Writing songs about painful relationships is a way for Taylor to connect with her fans, because most people have experienced a break up or have been hurt by love. Hearing songs about other people's pain helps the healing process.

"The hardest thing about heartbreak is feeling like you're alone, and that the other person doesn't really care," Taylor told *Seventeen*. "But when you hear a song about it, you realize you're not alone—because the person who wrote it went through the same thing. That's why songs about heartbreak are so relatable. When you miss somebody, and you hear a *happy* song, it just makes you mad."

Taylor said she will never stop writing heartbreak songs, because loss and love are such prevalent themes in life. "As human beings, what we can't have is what we replay in our head over and over again before we go to sleep," she told *Allure*.

All about Her Fans

Songwriting may help Taylor cope with upset, but she still feels bad or alone at times. "Usually, when life is happening to you, you feel like you're the only one going through it," she explained. "When I finish a song, sometimes I think 'I must be the only person who has ever felt this way, right?'"

Wrong. Thanks to her fans, Taylor soon learned she wasn't alone in her feelings. At signings, concerts and on MySpace and Facebook, her fans often say her songs helped them get through a break up or simply lifted their spirits. What Taylor writes in a song often mirrors what her fans are going through in life. "You don't imagine when you're writing a song in your living room that it's going to go out in the world and affect somebody you've never met," Taylor said.

It's a dream come true for Taylor, who always hopes her music helps people, no matter the person's age or situation in life. "I stand for the girl who is 15 and is in school and doesn't fit in. Maybe she can find some sort of comfort by going home and putting on my CD," Taylor said. "Or for the mother and daughter who don't get along—but maybe when they listen to my music, they do. Or you know, a cute couple who didn't have a song, but they listen to one of my songs and that becomes their song."

Connecting with fans—through music, lyrics and experiences—is of utmost importance to Taylor, and it's another reason she's been so successful. She even wrote about this connection on her MySpace page: "You stand there, singing those lyrics and writing them all over your car windows and your shirts," she said. "And I want you to know that it makes me so happy, because it's reassurance that we're all connected somehow. And I really love knowing that."

Her lyrics have touched millions of people, and that's something Taylor does not take for granted. The first time she wrote an album, she didn't know if people would care about what she had to say. Writing her *Fearless* album, however, was a bit different; by then, she knew her fans would know her lyrics by heart. "It makes it all worthwhile," she said.

Taylor often hugs her fans at events and takes photos with them. She strikes up conversation and tries to looks her fans in the eye. That's because she remembers, not that long ago, being in their exact position. "I went to concerts, and I went through meet-and-greet lines, and I know what it's like to walk away and think that you didn't really make an impression on your favorite artist and that you were kind of just in a line," she said. "I never want anyone leaving my concert feeling like I didn't appreciate them coming with everything that I have."

She has even become friends with some of her fans. "If we strike up a conversation and we like the same things and we have the same sense of humor, then they're my friend," she told *Self*. "It doesn't matter how I met them."

Taylor takes her relationship with her fans seriously, and she's tries to be there for them emotionally and even physically when they suffer. She said when something tragic happens to a fan, she cries very hard. "I've sat there in the bus with the family of an eighteen-year-old who got in a car wreck and died his senior year, who had my CD cover taped to the dash of his car," she said.

Taylor demonstrated this dedication to her fans when she made a special appearance on the finale of *The Oprah Winfrey Show* in May 2009. The show was about "The World's Most Talented Kids," and Oprah's co-host was Jordan, a talented 10-year-old and big Taylor Swift fan. Oprah told Jordan that Taylor Swift sent her a signed guitar, and the girl began to scream. "Guys, bring it out," Oprah said. But it was Taylor Swift herself who brought the guitar out to

"You don't imagine when you're writing a song in your living room that it's going to go out in the world and affect somebody you've never met," Taylor said.

"I've never needed an escape like drinking or drugs or anything like that to escape from the bad days," she told Entertainment Weekly. "Music has always been that escape for me."

MySpace is **Your Space**

■ Taylor Swift spends about 30 minutes online every day. When she's on the Internet, it's usually to update her MySpace page, which has become a spot for her to chat about important things like award nominations or performances and less important things, like the fact that she carried a tube of Pillsbury cinnamon rolls in her purse in case she got a chance to bake during the day.

She keeps her page personal because she wants people to see she's a regular person. "When I first started doing MySpace, I wrote my bio in the first person," she explained. "I didn't want my MySpace page to look like a publicity promo site, so I was the one doing all the commenting, and I was the one putting up pictures and videos."

A specialist actually makes the videos now, but she's the one who edits them. These clips show the many sides of Taylor Swift. In one, she's touring Australia, where she actually held a koala bear. In another, she's driving a golf cart around the parking lot of an arena with her mom.

Taylor holds a special place in her heart for her MySpace fans. "The people who go to my Myspace page are the people who make me happiest," she told *Self*. "That's why I like to make videos

for them. I like to thank them as much as possible."

With millions of friends on MySpace, Taylor makes time to respond to her fan's comments. She also lists

her fans' websites on her page. That's because her fans help her feel good about herself.

"Going on MySpace immediately makes my day better. I may be thinking 'My hair doesn't look right', 'I don't like this outfit', or 'I need to do this or that'," she said. "But when I log in, they're like 'You're music has changed my life,' 'Your music got me through this break up,' 'Your song means so much to me.' When people are just constantly being loving to you, it's the nicest thing. It's just so cool. It's a constant stream of love."

a stunned Jordan. Taylor hugged Jordan and told her she was "awesome." Oprah then gave Jordan a special assignment: interview Taylor Swift on her *Fearless* tour.

Taylor knows she would not have been successful without her fans like Jordan, those who buy her albums, download her songs, vote for her for awards, and visit her websites. She shows them how much she cares by giving them 100% of her time and energy when she's on the road. She once signed autographs for nine hours straight.

Good Girl

Because she values her fans, Taylor tries to display a positive image in all aspects of her life. Her strong moral character and integrity have won over the hearts of young girls and their parents.

Taylor believes it's her responsibility to be a good role model for young women, and that means saying no to underage drinking. It isn't hard for Taylor to refrain from partying. It was never something she liked to do.

"On weekends, my friends were starting to party already, and steal alcohol from their parents. I was never even tempted," she said of her days in junior high school. While her friends experimented with drugs and alcohol, she performed at karaoke bars and festivals.

"I've never needed an escape like drinking or drugs or anything like that to escape from the bad days," she told *Entertainment Weekly*. "Music has always been that escape for me."

In other words, music saved Taylor from trying drugs and alcohol. Now that she's a star, her fans keep her on her best behavior. "Knowing that there are thousands of little girls who have my album and watch how I behave is really a great thing for me," she told *Seventeen*. "Every time I'm faced with a decision or a choice, I think about the 6-year-old girl in the front row of my concert, and what she'd think about it. Then I think about her mom, and what she'd think. I never lose sight of what's really im-portant. To me, it's those girls."

Taylor has other valid reasons for not drinking alcohol. She said she always wants to be in control of what she does and says, and she wouldn't want to lie to her parents. Trust is very important to Taylor. "When you lose someone's trust, it's lost, and there are a lot of people out there who are counting on me right now," she said.

She's also witnessed the negative effects of partying. "When I was in high school, I remember seeing girls crying in the bathroom every Monday about what they did at a party that weekend," she said. "I never wanted to be that girl crying in the bathroom."

Being a good role model has its disadvantages. Many times, Taylor has not attended a party given by friends because she feared being connected with underage drinking. "Your career could go up in smoke just like that," she noted. "It's not worth the risk."

It's a smart decision for Taylor. Many young stars—Lindsay Lohan, Paris Hilton, and Britney Spears, to name a few—have dealt with bad publicity in recent years. In an age of bad behavior, Taylor has made a name for herself by being a good girl. It's a virtue her fans' parents appreciate. In

Starring **Taylor Swift**

Most musicians appear in their own music videos, but not all of them act in them. Taylor Swift has taken a very active part in her music videos, playing the female role in whatever story she tells. It's just another way she makes herself available to her fans. Here's a rundown of the parts she's played in a few of her award-winning videos:

"Love Story": Dressed in a period costume—a corset top dress; a few strands of hair falling down in tendrils—she plays Juliet, who meets her Romeo at a formal dance and longs for him afterward from her balcony.

"White Horse": Taylor plays the sad girl who finally realizes her boyfriend is not Prince Charming. She gives a heart-wrenching performance, complete with tears and an upsetting phone conversation.

"You Belong with Me": Look closely, Taylor plays two roles in this video. She's the nerdy girl with glasses in love with her next-door neighbor *and* the jerky cheerleader girl-friend. (She's wearing a sleek brown wig.) Parts of the video were filmed at Pope John Paul II High School in Hendersonville, Tennessee, where Taylor's brother attended. Her crush is played by Lucas Till, who also appeared in *The Hannah Montana: The Movie* as Miley Stewart's love interest.

"Every time I'm faced with a decision or a choice, I think about the 6-year-old girl in the front row of my concert, and what she'd think about it."

Like country singer Carrie Underwood, Taylor promotes a positive image for young girls.

"I've never wanted to use my age as a gimmick, as something that would get me ahead of other people," Taylor said." I've wanted the music to do that."

Taylor's good friend, Miley Cyrus, also embraces her youth while working in the music industry.

fact, mothers often approach Taylor at events to say, "You're what I hope my daughter grows up like."

This kind of response from parents means the world to Taylor. "That's the best compliment you could give me because it's about my character, which to me is the biggest honor," she said. "I always try to operate by the standards that I set for myself, because those standards are the hardest to beat."

Taylor wants to keep this trend, so she's made some hefty vows not to end up like those other stars. In several interviews, she said she has never smoked a cigarette or drank alcohol, and she promises not to drink until she is 21 years old. "I'm going to stay on course and not fall off the deep end," she told *USA Weekend*. "I don't want to end up in rehab. I promise you that I won't."

Keepin' it Real

Taylor is also very honest, especially about who she is. She was raised to be true to herself, and that often means being sincere. She never tries to act older or more mature, she said.

"I don't like it when people who are young act like they're 40. That's taking too much on," she told *The Washington Post*. "Some people might say I'm mature for my age, but it's not something I'm trying to do, you know? I'm just me."

Taylor may embrace her youth, but she tries not to make an issue of it. She hasn't hidden her age, but she also hasn't used it to her advantage "I've never wanted to use my age as a gimmick, as something that would get me ahead of other people," she said." I've wanted the music to do that."

Her age has actually been an obsta-cle, she said. At times, she felt like she had to prove something to the music industry or middle-aged listeners because she was so young. But for Taylor, part of being "yourself" is not worrying what other people think of you, and she tries not to concern herself too much with her image. "Some people see me as a kid, some people see me as an adult," she said. "But I'm seriously not going to complain how anybody sees me, as long as they see me."

Determination & Dedication

Taylor Swift's life—when she's on the road—can be very hectic. It's something she's put up with since the beginning. "I once went on the most grueling radio tour," she said. "Living in hotel rooms, sleeping in the backs of rental cars as my mom drove to three different cities in one day."

Since then, she's acquired a tour bus with all the comforts of home (see the Chapter 8 sidebar "Inside Taylor's Tour Bus"). Her schedule, however, remains full. "I'll take a red-eye and do an interview, then go to a meet-and-greet, then do an appearance, then get ready for a show, then do a conference call about the album," she told *Women's Health*. "My brain does get fried, but I never get tired of this."

She doesn't get tired because she's very determined and dedicated to her music. And this commitment is what has made her so successful, suggested Scott Borchetta. "Music comes first—it's music-business, not business-music," he said.

Looking back at her childhood—when she dropped off demo tapes or sang at every karaoke contest in the county—it's no wonder Taylor is fo-cused. Her mom remembered this determination from a young age. "She's just very sure of who she is," Andrea Swift told *Entertainment Weekly*. "She's been that way since she was tiny. I don't know why—it's nothing I did, and when I was her age, I was doing everything I could do to fit in. It's not stubbornness, just sureness. And she's self-governed because she chooses to be."

Taylor chooses to focus on her music because music is her life. She puts it before everything—even having a boyfriend—because her schedule does not allow her to date much. Music is part of who she is.

"Maybe this makes me sound like a robot, but there is nothing more interesting to me than my career," she said. "I feel sooooo lucky to have found something I love sooooo much. I don't have an identity without music. It probably sounds crazy, but I want to do everything I can to keep this precious thing intact."

To keep things intact, she remains humble and keeps music at the heart of her career. She tries not to get caught up in her fame, so much that it changes who she is or the songs she writes. The fact that she was the best-selling artist in 2008—beating out the Jonas Brothers and Miley Cyrus—is something that still blows her mind.

"I've been trying to do this all my life," Taylor said. "I remember the girls who would come to talent shows and say to anyone they met, 'I'm so-and-so—I'm going to be famous someday.' I was never that girl. I would show up with my guitar and say, 'This is a song I wrote about a boy in my class.' And that's what I still do today."

Chapter Four

Boy Story

No book about Taylor Swift would be complete without a chapter on boys. After all, the opposite sex has provided many moments of inspiration for the songwriter, who puts the names of her ex-crushes and ex-boyfriends into the lyrics of her songs. That's how Taylor processes her anger, a feeling she believes is only natural after a break up.

"I think getting mad is always your first reaction when something hurts. And you shouldn't feel bad about that," she told *Seventeen*. "Every person you date is different and makes you feel differently. Sometimes you can shake it off and you're fine—and then with another person it can really affect you. It's the unpredictability of love that really scares us, but it's also what draws us into it."

Love has definitely captured Taylor Swift, as evidenced by her song topics of boys and relationships. It seems Taylor is a hopeless romantic. "I have always been fascinated with fairy tales and the idea that Prince Charming is just one castle away," she told *Allure*. "And you're gonna run across a field and meet each other in the middle, and have an amazing, perfect movie kiss. And it's all gonna be happily ever after."

It's hasn't been happily ever after for Taylor, though. She's had crushes on boys who haven't liked her in return. "I'm the girl who—I call it girl-next-door-itis—the hot guy is friends with, and gets all his relationship advice from, but he never considers dating," she admitted to *Teen Vogue*.

She's also had her heart broken and endured upsetting break ups. But being a songwriter, she's used these moments of pain to ignite her music. Working the names of ex-boyfriends into the lyrics is a small form of revenge for Taylor, as illustrated by the liner notes of the deluxe edition of her self-titled album. Along with a long list of thank yous, she included this line: "To all the boys who thought they would be cool and break my heart, guess what? Here are 14 songs written about you. HA!"

Teardrops on My Guitar

Taylor's first big crossover hit was "Teardrops on My Guitar." The lyrics describe a girl in love with a boy unaware of her feelings: "Drew looks at me/I fake a smile so he won't see/What I want and what I need/And everything that we should be."

Taylor Hanson, the middle brother of the band Hanson, was Taylor Swift's childhood crush.

Who is Taylor Crushing On?

Like most teenage girls, Taylor has crushed on hunky actors and musicians. Below are a few of the guys Taylor has liked from afar:

Childhood Crush: Taylor Hanson of the boy band trio Hanson. She liked him because they shared a first name.
Musical Crush: Justin Timberlake, the pop music star formerly of 'N Sync
TV Show Crush: Jeffrey Dean Morgan, who played Denny on *Grey's Anatomy*
Fellow Country Singer Crush: Stephen Barker Liles of the band Love and Theft
Dream Date Crush: Chace Crawford of *Gossip Girl*
International Crush: The Irish singer-songwriter Danny O'Donaghue of The Script.

Taylor called Justin Timberlake her musical crush; he even surprised her with a visit on The Ellen DeGeneres Show.

Taylor posed with Nick, Joe, and Kevin Jonas at the 2008
MTV Video Music Awards. It was rumored she was dating

That girl, of course, is Taylor Swift. During Taylor's freshman year at Hendersonville High School, she fell hard for a boy named Drew. "He had the most beautiful eyes and amazing smile," Taylor said of Drew. "He was so cute and nice—and he talked to me every day...about his girlfriend! Which is like the screeching brake sound. But I had it bad for him. And I just kept thinking 'Why am I so invisible to him? Why does he have to have a girlfriend?'"

Taylor never told Drew how she felt; instead, she poured her feelings into the song "Teardrops on My Guitar." Eventually, Drew took the hint and showed up unexpectedly at Taylor's house. "It would have been really cool and poetic if he had turned up at my house right after my album came out," she explained. "But it was two years later."

Two years after the release of her self-titled album, Drew appeared in her driveway during the holidays. Taylor was just leaving to attend a hockey game with her friends Carrie Underwood and Kellie Pickler. After her dad said, "Hey, there's someone here to see you," she was surprised to find Drew standing there, waiting to talk to her. "It was like in the movies where at the end the guy shows up in your driveway, and you have this awesome kiss—except it's three years too late," she said. "I'm like, 'Why didn't you do this years ago?' He was a stranger by then, so I felt like I didn't know him anymore."

At that point, so much had happened in Taylor's life, and she had changed as a person. She no longer felt the same for Drew. She was over him because she'd already vented her feelings through the song. "I was like,

'It's really great to see you. But you're a little late,'" she said.

Taylor later told *Florida Entertainment Scene* that, after the awkward moment in the driveway, Drew called her five times. "I let those go to voice-mail," Taylor said. "Sometimes it's just too little, too late."

The "Other" Drew

Coincidentally, there were two boys named Drew in Taylor's life that first year of high school. Unlike her crush named Drew, this one she dated for some time. He was three years older, a senior, and he played hockey. "We weren't an 'It' couple," Taylor said of the relationship. This Drew, however, inspired two of Taylor's romantic hits, "Our Song" and "Tim McGraw."

Taylor wrote "Our Song" for the ninth grade talent show. At that time, she and Drew did not have a song to call their own, so she wrote one for them. If the lyrics are true, then Taylor and Drew spent many nights talking on the phone late at night. Taylor also went to Drew's prom that spring; they had their picture taken before the big night in his backyard.

That summer, Taylor spent time with Drew, but the relationship ended when Drew went off to college. It was hard for Taylor to say good-bye, and when she looked back on the relationship, she thought of one thing she'd remember most: Tim McGraw. Of course, this was Taylor's inspiration for her first hit single "Tim McGraw"; the two lovebirds had spent the summer listening to Tim McGraw songs. "Can't Tell Me Nothin'" is Taylor's favorite Tim song. In fact, the song title is the phrase she encoded in the CD jacket lyrics for the song "Tim McGraw."

Taylor said she has "totally moved on" when it comes to her ex-boyfriend Drew. "Drew's a great guy," she admitted, "but we're not really in touch."

Drew admitted, however, to buying Taylor's self-titled album featuring the two songs he inspired. "He really loved it, which is sweet," she said. "His current girlfriend isn't too pleased with it, though."

Bad Cheater Guy

Taylor obviously had a healthy relationship with Drew, but she would soon experience heartbreak when she met a boy named Sam. "He's the guy who made the unfortunate error of cheating on a songwriter," Taylor told *Blender*. "Big Mistake."

It was a mistake because Taylor went on to write "Should've Said No" about Sam. The lyrics are a rant against the boy who cheated on her: "And I should've been there in the back of your mind/I shouldn't be asking myself why/You shouldn't be begging for forgiveness at my feet/You should've said no, baby and you might still have me."

Taylor might have considered giving Sam another chance but decided not to; she believed she was worthy of more. "There's always that moment where you're like 'he says he's not gonna do it again, he says he's sorry, and oh, look how sorry he is! But they're not sorry," she told *Seventeen*. "If they cheated on you, then you didn't matter enough for them to be thinking about you while it was happening. So what does it matter if he apologizes after the fact? And at some point, you realize you do not deserve to be treated like that. I decided I didn't want to be that *that* girl."

According to Entertainment

One Boy Who'll Never Break Taylor's Heart

■ There is one boy who could never break Taylor's heart: her brother. Austin Swift, who is about two years younger than Taylor, is one guy with whom Taylor shares a great relationship.

"We used to fight like cats and dogs," Taylor said. "But when I went on the road, I started really missing him. I'd come back and he'd be four inches taller. So we started hanging out when I came home."

Austin attended John Paul II High School in Hendersonville, where he played lacrosse. He has different interests when it comes to music. Taylor called his taste "eclectic and cool."

"He introduced me to Kings of Leon, things I wouldn't have ventured into," she said. "He likes Jack White. He's into the coolest production and how does that sound, and I'm all about words."

Like Taylor, Austin is smart. He earned good grades in school. He doesn't, however, plan to follow in his big sister's footsteps. "He doesn't want to do music," Taylor said. "He's the opposite (of me.)"

Austin loves his sister, but it seems he needs his own space at times. He moved into a room on the garage level of the Swift house, perhaps to find a small respite from his sister's success.

Taylor's brother, Austin, introduced her to bands like Kings of Leon.

Weekly, Taylor referred to Sam as "Bad Cheater Guy." She actually got revenge on him twice. The lyrics are telling, but so is the secret message she put in the CD jacket of her self-titled album. She encoded Sam's name over and over in the lyrics of the song.

"It was only his first name, but everyone figured it out," Taylor divulged to *Women's Health.* "I'd get texts from him. He was scared out of his mind I'd crucify him on a talk show. All I could think was, 'Well, you *should've* said no.' That's what the song is about."

Although Sam seemed concerned about being publicly humiliated by Taylor, it's probable he secretly liked being named in her song. "Those kinds of guys like getting attention—because I mean, what else is he doing?" Taylor pondered. "He's probably with six different girls who don't know that they're being played."

It's unclear who Taylor's song "Picture to Burn" is about, but the song resembles "Should've said No" in theme. The song describes a bad relationship with a "redneck" who wouldn't let Taylor drive his truck: "And so watch

me strike a match/On all my wasted time/As far as I'm concerned/You're just another picture to burn."

There are two messages in "Picture to Burn." One goes out to the jerky ex-boyfriend, and the other goes out to the girls who listen to Taylor's songs. She gives them a piece of advice in the encoded message of the CD jacket lyrics: "Date Nice Boys."

Say It Ain't So, Joe

Perhaps Taylor's most public boyfriend was Joe Jonas, the middle brother of Disney's Jonas Brothers.

The two probably met through mutual friends and professional circumstances. Taylor's gal pal Miley Cyrus dated Nick Jonas, and Taylor's other good friends, Demi Lovato and Selena Gomez, also star on Disney television shows. Taylor also made an appearance in *Jonas Brothers: The 3D Concert Experience*, a concert film released in February 2009.

In the summer of 2008, the media speculated Taylor and Joe were dating, but the relationship wasn't confirmed until after it ended that fall. During the two-month courtship, neither Taylor nor Joe spoke to the press, but rumors spread when the two were seen together at the 2008 MTV VMAs. They were also photographed outside of Tao, a trendy Asian restaurant in New York's Midtown. Additionally, Taylor was seen in the front row of Joe's concert and vice versa. The two are almost the same age; Joe is about four months older than Taylor.

"He's an amazing guy, and anyone would be lucky to be dating him," was all Taylor said of Joe Jonas at the time.

A few months later, Taylor sang a different tune about the boy heart-throb famous for his deep-set eyes and thick eyebrows. On November 11, 2008, Taylor appeared on *The Ellen DeGeneres Show* for a release party for her *Fearless* album. That day, she opened up to host Ellen DeGeneres about her break up with Joe Jonas.

"That guy's not in my life anymore, unfortunately," Taylor said, after Ellen put a picture of Joe Jonas up on the in-studio screen. "That's an 'ouch.'"

Taylor divulged to Ellen that "Forever & Always," track number 11 on her *Fearless* album, was about her relationship with Joe Jonas. After a

> *"When I find that person who is right for me...he'll be wonderful. And when I look at that person, I'm not even gonna be able to remember the boy who broke up with me over the phone in 25 seconds when I was 18."*

last-minute recording session, Taylor added the song to the CD just before it came out.   She also admitted she hadn't talked to Joe Jonas since the break up, but she was "cool" with everything.

"When I find that person who is right for me...he'll be wonderful," Taylor told Ellen and the studio audience. "And when I look at that person, I'm not even gonna be able to remember the boy who broke up with me over the phone in 25 seconds when I was 18."

The crowd went wild when Taylor dropped the juicy news that Joe Jonas had broken up with her over the phone. "No, you did not," Ellen replied, waving her hand through the air and snapping with attitude.

Taylor, who remained quite composed despite the audience's reaction, offered up a few more details. "I looked at the call log, and it was like 27 seconds," Taylor recalled of the phone call. "That's got to be a record."

After the the show, Taylor made another jab at Joe Jonas. This time, she posted a video on her MySpace page. In it, she held two dolls, one of Joe Jonas and one of herself. "See, this one even comes with a phone. See? So he can break up with other dolls," she said about the boy doll. To the girl doll, she gave a stern command: "Stay away from him, okay?"

So why did Joe Jonas break up with Taylor Swift? In September, shortly after breaking up with Taylor, Joe Jonas began dating actress Camilla Belle, who starred in the film "*10,000 B.C.*" The two met during the filming of the Jonas Brothers' "Lovebug" video. At the time, it was rumored Joe cheated on the 18-year-old Taylor with the 21-year-old Camilla, but Joe claimed that was not true.

"I never cheated on a girlfriend," he wrote to his fans via the Jonas Brothers' blog. "It might make someone feel better to assume or imply I have been unfaithful, but it is simply not true. Maybe there were reasons for a break up. Maybe the heart moved on. Perhaps feelings changed. I am truly saddened that anything would potentially cause you to think less of me."

No matter what happened, Taylor got over Joe Jonas the same way she got over the others, by writing a song. She wrote "Forever & Always" in time to sneak it on to her *Fearless* album. "I'd never had that happen to me before that way, with that abruptness. I thought to myself, 'This needs to be said,'" Taylor explained. "It's a song about watching somebody completely fade away in a relationship and wondering what you did wrong and wondering why things have changed."

Like some of Taylor's other songs, the lyrics of "Forever & Always" are honest and aggressive: "Did I say something way too honest/That made you run and hide like a scared little boy?" Writing this feisty tune may have helped Taylor cope with the breakup, but she still experienced her share of sadness. "I have good days and I have bad days," she told *People* magazine post-breakup. "I'm trying to limit those days where I wake up and all I think about is that."

At first, Taylor wasn't ready to date again. She wanted to be alone and write about the ordeal. "I would hate to jump into something so quickly and have it not be the right thing, because I don't think I could take that right now," she said at the time.

Unfortunately, she did have to face Joe Jonas on December 31, 2008; the two both made guest appearances on *Dick Clark's Rockin' New Year's Eve Show*. On the brighter side, though, it was reported that Joe Jonas was unable to take a role in the film *Valentine's Day*, which Taylor starred in opposite *Twilight* star Taylor Lautner. That was definitely an awkward moment avoided.

Call it poetic justice, but the relationship between Joe and Camilla didn't last anyway. After dating almost a year, the two broke up "on good terms" in July 2009, according to Camilla's publicity representative.

Stephen

Sometimes, even Taylor Swift has a hard time telling a boy she likes him. So, when she had a crush on 24-year-old Stephen Barker Liles of the country band Love and Theft, she decided to tell him in a song. It seems he's the inspiration for the tune "Hey, Stephen" on her *Fearless* album.

"It's someone who I've always been friends with," Taylor said of the boy

Stephen Barker Liles, the lead singer of the band Love and Theft, was the inspiration for Taylor's song "Hey Stephen."

named Stephen. "And always kind of had a thing for...and he doesn't know."

Taylor never confirmed that the Stephen in the song is the lead singer of Love and Theft, but she did encode the name of his band in the lyrics of the song, which can hardly be a

coincidence.

Taylor met Stephen in 2007, while backstage during an event. Although the two have gotten closer since then—his band opened for her on tour—they never actually dated. "Sometimes all it takes to write a song about someone is thinking that they're cute," Taylor explained to *People*.

It seems Taylor thought Stephen was more than just cute. The lyrics describe the exhilaration of having a crush: "Cause I can't help it if you look like an angel/Can't help it if I wanna kiss you in the rain so/Come feel this magic I've been feeling since I met you/Can't help it if there's no one else/ Mmm, I can't help myself."

Taylor knew Stephen would hear the song; in fact, that was the fun part of putting it on the album. "It's always fun for me to put something on the album that is personal," she said. "Something I know I'm going to have to deal with when it comes out."

Ellen Cheers Up Taylor

■ While Taylor revealed the details of her breakup with Joe Jonas on *Ellen*, the show's host found many ways to make Taylor laugh. Ellen DeGeneres was sympathetic about the breakup, saying it must be hard to cope when the other person is so visible.

Taylor agreed. "He's on like pencil sharpeners and T-shirts," she said. "There's also a doll."

To this, Ellen replied, "I bet you have that with some pins or something."

Of course, Taylor laughed along with the audience before saying, "Someday, I'm going to find someone really, really great who's right for me."

"You're 18 years old...you're gonna find about 40 people who are right for you," Ellen spat back. "What about Nick? Go for another brother. That will get him back, if you go for one of the brothers. Or Kevin. There's two other brothers to go to."

This made Taylor laugh so hard, she bent over and put her hand over her mouth. She laughed again when Ellen asked if she planned to drive by Joe Jonas' house. Taylor is known for driving by the houses of her ex-boyfriends.

"He's got a lot of security guards,' Taylor said of Joe Jonas. "They're big. So probably not."

Ellen really cheered Taylor up later in the show. In fact, Taylor's mouth dropped wide open when she received a surprise visit from pop singer Justin Timberlake, who Taylor had deemed her "musical crush."

When Justin came out, Taylor shouted "No Way!" several times. "This makes it all better," she said after she was seated comfortably beside Justin on the couch.

Ellen soon tried to bring Justin into the conversation about Joe Jonas. "Why are men such jerks, Justin?" she asked.

"Well...where do I start?" Justin replied a bit tongue-tied. "You ladies are just smarter than us. See, I've accepted that. I'm much more comfortable in my stupidity...so that makes me less of a jerk."

"That's the best surprise ever," Taylor suddenly exclaimed, in awe of Justin's presence. "This is the best day ever."

Comedian and talk show host Ellen DeGeneres cheered Taylor up after her breakup with Joe Jonas.

Love on Tour?

■ Taylor's music appeals to both females and males, and the boy fans have certainly made their love of her known. One boy got her signature tattooed on his arm. Another pair of boys wore T-shirts that read, "Marry me, Juliet" to an event. Often times, men will call out "Marry me" during quiet moments at her concerts. Of course, Taylor is always flattered by the attention, but has she ever actually dated one of her fans? Believe it or not, she came close.

Once, when she was signing autographs at a college, she noticed a good-looking guy across the field who looked like Jeffrey Dean Morgan, the actor who played Izzie's tragic love interest Denny on *Grey's Anatomy*. "I was so obsessed with Denny from *Grey's Anatomy*, and he died, and he was my favorite, and I have this weird obsession with

that character," Taylor explained to *Rolling Stone*. "So this guy and I made eye-contact from across this field and I had a line of people that were waiting to get autographs and he waited at the end of the line and came through the line. We made small talk and I was talking to him and he held out a picture for me to sign, and I just grabbed his hand and wrote my number down."

Taylor insisted that was the only time she'd ever tried to pick up one of her fans. "But he looked so much like Denny, come on!" she argued in her defense.

In the end, nothing happened with the Denny look-a-like. "I didn't follow through," Taylor said. "I think I was like, 'Get a hold of yourself! You just wrote your number on a stranger's hand. Get yourself together.'"

Taylor almost dated one of the fans she met while signing autographs at a college.

So what did Stephen think of the song? Obviously, he was flattered, but said he and Taylor are just friends. He does, however, think highly of her. "I think everyone would agree she's a total sweetheart and anyone would be lucky to go out with her," he said.

Here's an interesting factoid about "Hey Stephen" that has nothing to do with love: country singer Martina McBride's kids actually served as guest performers on the track. "We were recording in her husband's

studio, and they were hanging out," Taylor explained to *USA Today*. "We just hauled them all into the studio, put a microphone on them and had them snap their fingers to the end of the song."

Worth the Pain

Taylor would never wish away the memory of a bad relationship, because those cheating boyfriends and redneck jerks helped catapult her career. Fortunately, Taylor processes her

anger and heartbreak through songwriting. "It's hard to get furious about it, because the only reason you're furious at them is because they don't love you," she said. "And when I get to that place, it's more my inclination to write about the sadness of that."

Taylor likes to believe that everything happens for a reason, and her songs help her make sense of her pain. "I'm the kind of person who needs everything to be justified and needs all of her time to be worth the energy," she said. "So, let's say I date a guy who really does nothing but damage me. And you've spent time, and you've spent effort, and you've put everything into trying to make that work. And it didn't. So you write a song about it. It was worth everything, if you write a song about it."

Her songs allow her to not only comment on her past relationships, but also send a departing message

Lessons Learned

With every heartache or crush that didn't turn into a relationship, Taylor Swift seems to have learned lessons about love, relationships, boys and even herself. She appreciates the positive aspects of a negative experience. "I think that you never fully let go of everything," she explained. "And that should be your goal, because you can take away something good from

she explained. "But the worst is when you think you finally went for the nice guy and he breaks your heart it's like, 'What gives?'"

If nice guys can turn out to be bad guys, then a girl must protect her heart when dealing with boys, especially the ones who play games. For this reason, Taylor advises her friends to play games too, if the guy they're dating is doing it. "You shouldn't start out playing games, but if he doesn't call you for two days, just 'forget' to call him for two days," she explained. "You just didn't have time to call because he didn't have time to think about your feelings. You have to out-play the player."

Taylor might have learned this approach from her mom, who gave her the best piece of advice about boys. "Don't ever call a guy first. The thing they want the most is whatever they can't have," Taylor said. "It sounds very juvenile, but it's true."

> ## "When someone breaks up with me, I like to write about it, because I feel like I have the last word," she told Rolling Stone. "That's the fun part."

to an ex-boyfriend. "When someone breaks up with me, I like to write about it, because I feel like I have the last word," she told *Rolling Stone*. "That's the fun part."

Taylor isn't heartless, though. She takes pity on these boys she has written songs about. "They move on to different relationships and their new girlfriends are smacking them in the car when the song comes on," she told *Entertainment Weekly*.

Could writing such honest songs about her ex-boyfriends ruin her chances with future boys? Will they assume she'll go on to write a song about them? When it comes to future relationships, Taylor stands her ground: "If you don't want me to write bad songs about you, then don't do bad things."

everything that happens to you."

Although she dreams about the perfect relationship, she realizes love is never perfect. "I have to believe in fairy tales, and I have to believe in love—but not blindly," she told *Seventeen*. "If you do meet Prince Charming, know he is going to have his good days and his bad days. He is going to have days when his hair looks horrible, and days when he's moody and says something that hurts your feelings. You have to base your fairy tale not upon happily ever after, but on happy right now."

Taylor has also learned that in love, things are not always as they seem. Good guys can break your heart too. "Bad boys know how to keep the chase going through the entire relationship, and you never know if you completely have them or not,"

In addition to playing the game, a girl should also read the warning signs when she sees them. One thing that scares Taylor away are boys who talk too much about their ex-girlfriends. It's a bad sign. "If they mention their ex-girlfriend within the first hour of conversation it's not going to go anywhere," she said. "It also says 'damaged' a little bit."

When a relationship does end, Taylor recommends walking away gracefully. She said she never wanted to be the lingering ex-girlfriend because she had to deal with these ex-girlfriends in the past. "I don't want to ruin his future relationships," Taylor explained to *Rolling Stone*. "And what if you're with someone great? You don't want to have lingering ex-boyfriend-itis."

"It's making yourself happy with your life that will attract people."

Taylor doesn't need to have a boyfriend; she seems at ease just hanging out with guys as friends. At the 2009 CMT Music Awards, Taylor posed with Ryan Keith Follese (Left) and Nash Overstreet (Right) of the band Hot Chelle Rae.

The Perfect Date

■ Taylor has traveled all over the United States, plus Canada, Australia, and the United Kingdom. So which location would she pick for the setting of the perfect date? Hendersonville, Tennessee. That's right, just like Dorothy from *The Wizard of Oz*, Taylor thinks there's no place like home.

"I live on a lake, so it's really fun to go out on the boat, and then hang out all night and just talk," she said while describing her idea of the perfect date. "It wouldn't have to be anything fancy or anything like that, but just being with a person who gets you. It's kind of funny because you don't have a lot of opportunities like that to be home and to go on a date in your hometown, but that's exactly what I would do."

When it comes to relationships, Taylor likes to keep the drama contained to her songs. She doesn't like to fight or get too upset when a relationship ends. "If he doesn't want to be with you, then let him do what he wants to do," she said. "The worst thing in the world to do is kick and scream and nag. The only time I lose my temper is in songs. I'm enthralled by relationships, and I love the drama in them, but that's usually where it lives. I'm not a dramatic person. I like to let people state their case before I get irrational about things."

Breakups hurt, but they won't sting as bad if you always keep your feelings in check. According to Taylor, a girl should be careful how deeply she falls for a boy. It shouldn't be so much that she'd be lost without him. Acting desperate is a real turnoff. "You should want the other person and love him, but you shouldn't need him," she said. "If you depend on him for your happiness, that's not good, because what will you do when it ends?"

In fact, it's okay not to have a boyfriend at all, said Taylor, who has seen many of her friends go from one boyfriend to the next looking for a love that lasts. If Taylor were to meet a great guy, she would date him. But if he's just mediocre, she might pass. "I've had those friends who have to have a boyfriend all the time, and as soon as it doesn't work out with one, they jump to another one within 24 hours," she said. "What would happen if you were stuck in a relationship with someone who wasn't right for you, just because you were lonely— and then missed meeting Mr. Right?"

Being Alone Is Not Lonely

Taylor admitted she's "never been the kind of girl who needs a boyfriend." She's okay with being single; she knows she's the only one responsible for her happiness. "Being alone is not the same as being lonely," she said. "When you're alone, you're going to have lonely moments, but it's important to be happy with yourself. Sure, you'll always feel a little weird being alone on Valentine's Day, but you can't let that force you into a relationship with a guy you're not supposed to be with."

Speaking of Valentine's Day, Taylor didn't have anyone special one year, so she wrote out 30 valentines to friends. This is just one of the ways she finds joy in being alone. According to Taylor, there are benefits to not having a boyfriend.

"I like to do things that glorify being alone," she noted. "I buy a candle that smells pretty, turn down the lights, and make a playlist of low-key songs. If you don't act like you've been hit by the plague when you're alone on Friday night, and just see it as a chance to have fun by yourself, it's not a bad day."

In fact, being confident without a boyfriend might actually make you more desirable to boys. "It's making yourself happy with your life that will attract people," she told *Cosmo Girl*. "If you don't seem lonely, that's when somebody's going to want you."

Music Is My Boyfriend

One reason Taylor is "perpetually single" is her career. With performances, tours and autograph signings, she's often too busy to have a boyfriend. That's just part of being a star; it's even something she and her good friend Kellie Pickler once talked about in Taylor's dressing room before a show.

"We can only give someone what's left over," Kellie told Taylor.

Taylor concurred. "She does the same thing I do, so she knows what it's like to do interviews all day and give your heart and soul on stage every night," she said of Kellie. "After all of that is taken, we can only give someone what's left. So it's hard."

Taylor's career requires a lot of her energy, time, and even her thoughts. Often, she's so concerned about her music, she doesn't even see opportunities for relationships. She's fascinated by her career not boys. Her friends will see guys who are cute, but Taylor doesn't. "I have these blinders on," she told the *Washington Post*. "It's not like I'm running out of time or what-

ever. But music is my boyfriend."

If she did have time for a boyfriend, she knows she would have to pick someone nice, someone her parents, friends and fans would accept. "I've got two million fans who are going to tell me if they don't approve of him, you know?" she said.

Any relationship Taylor could have would need to be long-distance due to her schedule. That's true even if the boy lived in Nashville, she said. "I'll be flying to see him and flying him places to see me. It feels like it would involve more scheduling, and I already deal with a lot of scheduling in my life," she said. "Of course, if I met somebody who was worth it, I would probably stop thinking that way!"

Meanwhile, Taylor's theory on love is to just let it happen naturally. It can be left to chance or fate; it will happen when you're not looking for it, she said.

"I'm not opposed to falling in love," she told *Teen Vogue*. "but I'm also not exactly out there looking."

Happily Ever After

So will Taylor ever meet Mr. Right? Will she ever get married? Or have her ex-boyfriends caused her to fall out of love with love? Taylor seems certain her happy ending is out there. "I'm going to meet somebody someday who is so wonderful, and I'm not even going to remember the other guys," she said. "Later on, I definitely want to fall in love and get married and have kids. I believe in love completely, wholeheartedly."

Although she sees marriage in her future, she doesn't want to get married for the sake of getting married. She said she would tie the knot only if "I find the person I absolutely can't live without." She admitted, however, that marriage is not her "ultimate goal in life."

If she does get married, she seems to know that personality and friendship mean as much, maybe even more, than good looks. "If you end up lasting with someone for years and years, eventually you'll run out of things to talk about or find out about each other," she explained. "So you'd better pick a person who can make you laugh about nothing, or who can pull conversations out of the air."

Taylor is still very young, and marriage may be many years away as she focuses on her career. But a new boyfriend may be in her future, if he can do one thing that makes him rise above the rest.

"When I find someone who fascinates me as much as my career," she said. "I'm gonna go for it."

What's Taylor's Type?

■ Taylor believes love is something that can't always be explained. "You can't predict who you'll fall in love with," she said. "Love's the one thing that doesn't have a pattern—it's a total mystery. If you over think it, you're wasting your time."

Taylor may believe in the magic of falling in love, but does she have a type? Not exactly. Taylor said it's unfair to have a specific idea of what the 'right' guy is like in regards to looks or personality. She sees boys as separate stories, not whole chapters in a book. However, she did mention one important quality.

"The guy I'm looking for is the guy I can be me around, not a version of me I think he'd like," she told *Seventeen*. "He's the guy I'm not wearing different clothes for. I'm not holding back jokes because he might think they're stupid. I'm not afraid to show emotion because I might scare him. It's important to not have rules about who the guy is: the rule should be about who you are when you're with him."

In other words, Taylor wants to be with someone who will like her no matter what, even if her hair is frizzy one day or her outfit is all wrong. "I've trained myself to think that personality is what counts, and that if I meet the right person on my worst day, it won't matter what I look like," she said.

Would she prefer to date someone famous, someone who understands life in the spotlight? Not necessarily. In the end, she wants someone who is secure with who he is.

"I think it's more a question of confidence. I wouldn't want to be with a pushover who would let me make all the plans and have all the control," she said. "It's really natural for me to go into planning mode, but I'd rather be with someone who has his own voice and passion and ambition."

Chapter Five

Friends Forever

Taylor has come a long way from those lonely days of adolescence, when she had no one to talk to or hang out with. Those mean girls from junior high are history. In fact, Taylor grew up to have meaningful, close friendships with women who understand her, support her, and love her for who she truly is inside.

Who are the friends she values most? When making friends, Taylor looks for a simple yet important characteristic. "I love people who are nice to me," she said. Despite her fame, Taylor isn't a snob about who can be her friend, and who can't. "All you need to do to be my friend is like me," she explained.

One might assume, because Taylor is a country and pop music sensation with millions of fans on both MySpace and Facebook, she has too many friends to count. Surprising, she only keeps a half dozen close friends, which she said is a lot for her. "It's weird—I thought I'd have so many more friends, but I feel like I'm less popular than I've ever been," she told *Teen Vogue*. "It makes me value the people I can trust even more."

My Mother, My Friend

One of Taylor's most trustworthy and closest friends is the woman who has always been there for her, literally from day one: her mother, Andrea Swift. Taylor's mom used to console Taylor in junior high when she cried about the mean girls at school. She also encouraged her to work hard for what she wanted.

"My mom is very rational," Taylor explained. "My mom always said, 'I don't feel like you just get discovered, there's a lot more that goes into it. I want you always to have high hopes but low expectations.'"

> "My mom always said, 'I don't feel like you just get discovered, there's a lot more that goes into it. I want you always to have high hopes but low expectations.'"

Unlike other parents Taylor witnessed growing up, Andrea Swift did not promise her daughter a future of fame. "Honey, I don't know if you're going to make it," Andrea said instead. "All you can do is try your hardest."

Taking her mom's advice, Taylor did try her hardest and wound up a superstar. Her mom has been along for the ride ever since. She is usually the parent who travels with Taylor to events and concerts, although her father tags along from time to time. Their mother-daughter relationship is unique.

"She's one of my best friends," Taylor said of her mom. "She's always, always around. She's the person in my life who will just literally look me in the eye and say, 'Look, snap out of it'... and I need that person."

Taylor and her mom may be best friends, but Andrea Swift never oversteps the boundaries of motherhood. Her mom has never tried to act cool or party with her teenage daughter. "We're definitely never gonna go clubbing together," Taylor announced.

Like a good mother, Andrea Swift keeps her daughter on schedule during her tour, but she seems to do it without annoying Taylor too much.

Taylor appreciates her mother's confidence and business savvy. "My mother is so not a momager," she said.

There have been moments of tension between mother and daughter, though. What do they argue about? The temperature on the tour bus. Andrea Swift likes it cool, claiming, "germs grow in warm temperatures." Conversely, Taylor likes it warm.

"She tries to turn me into an ice cube," Taylor wrote on her MySpace blog. To keep this power play going, Taylor will turn the thermostat back up to 80 degrees when her mom is not watching.

Sometimes, Taylor doesn't mind her mother's meddling. Once, while she was visiting Los Angeles, Taylor came home to find her mother had rearranged her bathroom. Taylor used to keep all of her cosmetics and products on the bathroom counter; it was always a mess. Her mother fixed the problem. "My bathroom is now a magical, wondrous place with cabinets for storing make-up and hooks on the door for holding scarves," she explained. "There are even drawers for my hair brushes and incredible little shelves for my towels. There are little windows in one of the dressers, and through it, I can see the candles I

*Taylor's mom, Andrea Swift, encouraged
Taylor to always try her hardest.*

Taylor saw those mean girls from junior high again at an autograph signing. But her enemies became her fans!

Whatever Happened to Those Mean Girls from Junior High?

■ Remember those girls in Wyomissing, Pennsylvania; the ones who "dumped" Taylor Swift from their lunch table and lied to her about going to the mall? Well, it turns out they grew up to be Taylor Swift fans.

About a year after her music career began, Taylor played a concert in her hometown. Those mean girls showed up, but it wasn't to boycott her concert. They were there as fans; they wore her T-shirts and asked for her autograph on their CDs. The girls waited three hours to see Taylor.

"It was bittersweet, because it made me realize that they didn't remember being mean to me, and that I needed to forget about it, too," explained Taylor.

Taylor let go of any grudges that day. She realized her adolescent pain and suffering were mere stepping stones on her musical journey. In fact, Taylor actually thanks her former classmates for mistreating her. "If I hadn't been so driven to music because I didn't have anyone to hang out with, if I hadn't written songs because I didn't have anyone to talk to, I wouldn't be sitting here right now," she said.

Although Taylor has lived in Hendersonville, Tennessee, since 2004, she still enjoys visits to her old stomping grounds. "When I come back to Pennsylvania and see the crowds and the landscape, it's such a rush," she said. "It just feels like home."

According to the *Reading Eagle*, the local newspaper in Wyomissing, Taylor stays in touch with only one friend from her childhood, a girl named Britany Maack. Apparently, the two keep in contact while Britany is at college.

used to have stashed randomly on the counter. Now they have their perfect little home, all gathered together in their tiny, organized sanctuary."

Most teenage girls would have viewed this bathroom renovation as an invasion of privacy, but not Taylor. "The moral of the story is...my mom is wonderful and we apparently share the same hobby: compulsively organizing and straightening up around the house whenever we're bored," she said.

In 2008, Taylor found a very heartfelt and public way to thank her mother for her love and support. She wrote the song "The Best Day" as a tribute to her mother, putting the song on her *Fearless* album. Andrea Swift cherishes the song; she still remembers the first time she heard it on Christmas Eve.

"She had made this edited music video," Taylor's mom explained. "I'm looking on the TV and this video comes up with this voice that sounds exactly like Taylor's. And I looked over at her, and she said, 'I wrote it for you, Mom.' And that's when I lost it. And—and I've lost it pretty much every time I've heard that song since."

Sometimes, Taylor's mom can't believe how fast her daughter has grown or how successful she's become. "I still sometimes see that little two-year-old in the backseat in the car seat," she told *Dateline NBC*.

Although Taylor's mom is known for being rational, she still has her silly moments. At Taylor's prom-themed party for "Our Song," Andrea dressed up like a nerdy chaperone. She pinned her hair back, wore buckteeth and black-framed, Coke-bottle glasses, and carried a sign that read, "No kissing on dance floor."

Now that's what you call a fun mom.

> *"She had made this edited music video," Taylor's mom explained. "I'm looking on the TV and this video comes up with this voice that sounds exactly like Taylor's. And I looked over at her, and she said, 'I wrote it for you, Mom.' And that's when I lost it."*

Abigail Anderson

When it comes to friends her own age, Taylor's very best friend is Abigail Anderson. She met the red-haired Abigail her freshman year in an English course at Hendersonville High School, and they've been friends ever since.

Like many teenage girls, Taylor and Abigail get silly when they're together. For instance, they like to talk in weird accents. During Christmas of their freshman year, they stayed up late to make prank phone calls; they called their friends, and proceeded to talk in funny voices from the film *Napoleon Dynamite*. That same holiday season, the two were so bored, they made a video for a song titled, "We're Just Two Cowgirls." Sporting country western hats, Taylor sang in an obnoxious, off-key drawl, while Abigail tapped on a drum.

The two have shared serious moments as well. After a slew of painful breakups, the girls always bonded and coped by driving by their ex-boyfriends' houses. One breakup made it into the lyrics of Taylor's song "Fifteen." When Abigail "gave everything she had to a boy who changed his mind," both of them cried about it.

The following summer, when the boy from the song tried to get back together with Abigail, Taylor was again there to help. She brought her friend to a special spot where the boy stood holding roses. The boy had created a large heart out of candles, which Taylor thought was sweet. Taylor even burned a CD for the boy to play that evening. "He wouldn't have known Abigail's favorite songs otherwise," she said.

Things have certainly changed since the two girls first started hanging out. Back then, in addition to talking about boys, they often discussed their plans for the future. Taylor dreamed of being a singer, while Abigail aspired to go to college on a swimming

"We talk all the time, almost every day," Taylor said of Selena. "She's just such a cool person because she's so real..."

scholarship. Only a few years later, the girls have each made her dream a reality. Taylor became the number one selling artist in 2008, and Abigail attends Kansas University on a swimming scholarship.

When she's not giving a concert or appearing at an award show, Taylor loves to visit Abigail at KU in Lawrence, Kansas. In fact, she told *The Oprah Winfrey Show* a visit to KU would be the perfect day off. "It's this little college town, and it's kind of fun because you always kind of wonder about the path you didn't take, and the path I didn't take was going to college," she said. "When I have days off, I like to go and visit Abigail and experience college without having to actually take tests and study."

According to Kansas University's newspaper, *The Kansan*, Taylor accompanied Abigail to a course called "Media and Society." Fifteen minutes after the class started, more than 20 people stood at the back of the auditorium to feast their eyes on Taylor Swift. In the lobby, a group of 50 people gathered, waiting for the class to end. They knew Taylor Swift was inside because they had received text messages from friends alerting them of the star's presence.

Although Taylor was on campus to visit her friend, she did sign auto-graphs after the class ended. She also took photos with fans, with her bodyguard close by.

Taylor's fame has caused problems like this in the past. She said sometimes a group of her friends will opt out of inviting her to dinner to avoid a scene. But Abigail seemed to understand the inevitable excitement over her friend's visit. "It's like a snowball effect," she said of the KU campus hype. "One person hears it, and spreads it all over the place."

In fact, Abigail has remained supportive of Taylor's career. She appeared in a few of Taylor's videos, and she made a surprise appearance on *The Ellen DeGeneres Show*, the same episode featuring Justin Timberlake. Abigail has found ways to separate herself from her famous best friend, however. She wears a nose ring, and even owns a pet snake.

The girls may have grown up, but they haven't grown apart. They still love to hang out during the holidays. They listen to music, paint, and talk, just like they did when they were 15. One of their favorite holiday traditions is watching the movie *Love Actually*. They still get silly sometimes too.

"We decided we needed to get more in the holiday spirit so we bought festive Christmas sweaters," Taylor

wrote on her MySpace blog during Christmas 2008. "Like the kind that have reindeer and Santa all over them. Hers lit up. I was jealous."

Best Friend in the Business

Taylor is friends with several famous female stars, but who would she say is her best friend in the business? Selena Gomez of Disney's *Wizards of Waverly Place*. Taylor hangs out with Selena whenever she visits Los Angeles.

"We talk all the time, almost every day," Taylor said of Selena. "She's just such a cool person because she's so real, and a lot of times people get to a level where they're famous and people know them, people recognize them and they become...less real."

Although it's easy to be swept away by Hollywood, Selena hasn't been changed by fame, said Taylor, who appreciates her friend's great sense of humor.

Selena feels the same about Taylor. "She's such a great person. I'm so lucky to have a friend like her," she said after she received a huge arrangement of flowers from Taylor on her 17th birthday. "She's very honest, and I look up to her. I love you, Taylor!"

The two girls like to listen to each other's music. Once, Selena posted "Jammin' to 'You Belong with Me' in the car" on her Twitter page.

Of course, Taylor responded with the same affection: "Selena Gomez, I miss you! Pretending the hairbrush is a mic and blasting 'Stop and Erase' in the dressing room."

"Stop and Erase" is one of the songs off Selena's album *Kiss and Tell*.

Taylor appreciates more than Selena's singing voice; she's a fan of her

acting talents as well. She attended the movie premiere for *Another Cinderella Story* in which Selena starred.

"That movie rules," Taylor said. "I was crying and laughing, and she's so awesome in it."

Miley Cyrus

Another friend who understands the pressures of fame is Miley Cyrus, the country crossover star known for her Disney TV show *Hannah Montana*. That's one reason Miley and Taylor Swift are good friends.

"We've completely been there for each other," Taylor said of her friendship with Miley during an interview on Ryan Seacrest's radio program. Taylor hangs out with Miley when she visits L.A., and Miley hangs out with Taylor when she visits Nashville.

Their friendship is based on understanding, but the girls try not to talk about life in the spotlight. "We try and keep it friends and not discuss business and publicity," Taylor said, according to MTV.com. "It's fun being able to be friends with someone who does the same thing that you do and not have that come into play."

Taylor and Miley are such good friends, Miley once lent Taylor her boyfriend at the time, Justin Gaston, for an evening. In November 2008, Miley attended the CMA Awards alone so her boyfriend could play Romeo for Taylor's performance of "Love Story." Justin was also featured in Taylor's video for the song.

"I'm flying solo tonight," Miley said at the award show "But that's OK, because it means my two best

You're a Good Friend, Taylor Swift!

■ Taylor relies on her friends for support in good times and in bad, but is she a good friend in return?

It seems Taylor is a good listener. She offers her friends advice when dealing with problems, especially boy troubles. "Talking to my friends about their dating lives is my number one hobby," Taylor divulged to *Seventeen*. "Which is really ironic because when I go to them and ask, 'What should I do?' they're like 'I don't know!' And I'm like 'When you and your boyfriend were fighting, I talked to you for two hours and told you all those things. Remember?'"

She also gives great gifts. Once, she sent birthday flowers to her gal pal Selena Gomez of *Wizards of Waverly Place*. The arrangement of flowers was so big, two men had to deliver it to Selena's dressing room! When it was Miley Cyrus' birthday, Taylor and a group of girls gave her a surprise birthday cake.

Taylor's gifts are not always sweet; some are very practical. Her favorite gift to give is mace, a pepper spray designed to fight off an assault. "I gave it to Demi Lovato and Kellie Pickler for their birthdays because I don't want anything to happen to them," Taylor told *Girl's Life*. "Demi loved it, and her dad loved it, too."

Taylor extends her generosity to strangers as well. "I like going through Starbuck's drive-thru and paying for the person behind, just because it's nice," she admitted.

Cheering her friends up is something Taylor also likes to do. When her backup singer Liz got a stuffy nose and sore throat, Taylor sent her an "I miss you" card. The front of the card featured a kitten with a sad face. "I feel like kitten cards make everything better, pretty much," Taylor wrote on her MySpace blog. "Then I put Craisins in the card. Not packaged, just loose Craisins in the card. So hopefully the combination of cute kittens and Craisins will bring Liz back to perfect health."

Taylor might take her job as a friend a bit too seriously at times. Since she's obsessed with crime-scene shows, it's no wonder she's also obsessed with medical research. "I like to read up on weird medical problems," she admitted on her Facebook profile, "so if one of my friends ever complains of a headache or stomachache, I'm probably going to spout off 12 different things that could be wrong with them, because I'm way paranoid."

friends are onstage at the same time!"

Soon, Miley got her own moment on stage with Taylor. The two showed off their singing talents at the 2009 Grammys when they sang a duet of Taylor's song "Fifteen." Taylor thought Miley would identify with the song. "I think it's cool, because when she was 15 she had a lot of things going on," Taylor said of the *Hannah Montana* star. "Lessons learned."

Miley agreed: "I was on tour when I turned 15," she said. "The lyrics are really inspiring...this song is pretty perfect for the Grammys."

The girls sang without much fanfare. They sat on simple stools, while Taylor played acoustic guitar. Although performing at the Grammys was a huge deal, Taylor remained calm, thanks to Miley. "We're friends, so anytime I'm performing with her, my nerves go away, 'cause she's always trying to make me laugh or is doing something ridiculous," Taylor said. "It's so fun to get up there with one of your friends."

Taylor is such a dedicated friend to Miley, she almost lost her cool with a reporter backstage at an event. After Taylor won Top Female Vocalist at the ACM Awards, a reporter approached her with upsetting questions about Miley.

"Honestly, Miley is a really good friend and an amazing person," Taylor told the reporter, staring him down.

In return, Miley stood up for Taylor after Kanye West interrupted her acceptance speech at the 2009 MTV VMAs. When Jay Leno asked Miley what her response to Kanye would have been, she was assertive. "I would have said 'Rude! Disrespectful!'"

Miley said. "And I think I would have had to tell him to, like, let me finish my speech, so I'm happy she got to do that."

Blonde Power

Sometimes in friendship, opposites attract. That's certainly true when it comes to Taylor Swift and Kellie Pickler.

"She's like a sister," Taylor told the *Reading Eagle* about the former *American Idol* star. "People say we're such opposites, but that's what makes us such good friends. She's incredibly blunt. I love that about her. If some guy has said or done something to me she doesn't like, she'll grab my cell phone and say, 'I'm deleting his number.'"

Kellie is equally appreciative of Taylor's friendship. She respects Taylor's work ethic. "I've not seen many people work as hard as Taylor," Kellie told *Rolling Stone*. "She's a very competitive girl, and those people go far."

Taylor met Kellie while on tour with Brad Paisley; both ladies served as opening acts for his *Bonfires & Amplifiers* tour. They got into some trouble on that tour, pranking Brad by wearing large tick costumes. They soon became very good friends and even songwriting partners. The two

actually wrote Kellie's song "The Best Days of Your Life" while on tour with Brad Paisley.

"This song came to be after a show," Taylor wrote on her MySpace blog. "Kellie came storming onto my bus, fuming about something one of her ex-boyfriends did. She was ranting and raving and going on and on about it, and I just said, 'Kellie, you're saying lyrics right now. The things you're saying are a song. Let's go write it.'"

They wrote the song in 30 minutes; for Taylor, the experience was unforgettable. "It was so cool jumping into someone else's feelings for a minute and writing from their perspective," she said. "It was like I was writing my very first song. Exhilarating!"

The two blondes may be opposites, but they often dress the same for events. "For some reason, we always end up wearing the same color to award shows," Taylor said. For example, they both wore sparkly silver dresses to the CMAs, black dresses to the AMAs, and pink ones to the ACMs. "If anyone was thinking that we do this on purpose so we can be matching in our pictures, we don't," Taylor said. "It just happens."

Even after Brad Paisley's tour ended, Taylor and Kellie remained friends.

> *"People say we're such opposites, but that's what makes us such good friends. She's incredibly blunt. I love that about her."*

*Taylor and Kellie Pickler are not only
friends, but also songwriting partners.*

That's probably because Kellie's bubbly personality has a positive effect on Taylor. "Seeing Kellie always brightens my day, because she's always got something funny to say," Taylor said. "She's my friend, not just an acquaintance. I'd do anything for her."

Kellie would do anything for Taylor, too. In fact, she and Carrie Underwood look out for Taylor as if she's their little sister. The two country stars came to Taylor's rescue one night after the three attended a Nashville Predators hockey game together. A suspicious-looking guy approached Taylor at a gas station, but Kellie scared him away, calling it an act of "total blonde power."

"Get away from her, you old man," Kellie yelled at the guy. "If you're still around when we finish filling up with gas, we'll make a hood ornament out of you!"

Taylor deserves this kind of support from Kellie. After all, Taylor takes Kellie's successes to heart. She actually cried after Kellie won "Breakthrough Video of the Year" at the 2008 CMT awards. "I can't even explain how unbelievable it was to see her win her first award," Taylor wrote on her MySpace blog. "We had no cell service in the arena, so as soon as the show was over and we left, Kellie was my first call."

Taylor often promotes Kellie's work on her blog. She posts updates on Kellie's career, whether it's about a new single, new album, new video, or a stunning performance.

Taylor thinks so highly of Kellie's musical ability, she asked her to be an opening act for her *Fearless* tour.

"It's gonna be hilarious to be on the road with her again," Taylor said before the tour began. "I can't wait to go over to her bus and hang out with her and all of her tiny little animals that she has rapidly acquired. Between the cat, the dog, the snake, and the monkey...it's going to be a trip. Or a zoo. Or both. I love her, and I'm so lucky she's coming out with me."

Friends or
Competitors?

■ Taylor Swift is friends with some big stars: Miley Cyrus, Selena Gomez, Demi Lovato, Kellie Pickler, Emma Stone of the movie "Superbad," and even pop singer songwriter Colbie Caillat.

With such famous and talented girlfriends, does Taylor ever get jealous? Are these girls her friends or competitors?

"I've always approached this from the place where I don't compete with other girls," Taylor told the *Associated Press* according to *The Insider.* "I don't compete with other people in the industry. I compete with myself."

Taylor knows that having friends is a lot more fun than competing with them. She's very appreciative of the friendship's she's made with these other female superstars.

"If I looked at every other girl in the entertainment industry as competition, my life would be really lonely," she said. "I wouldn't have some of the coolest friends that I'm so glad I've gotten to know over the last couple of years.... It's really awesome to get to hang out with those girls and to call them friends."

Taylor and Emma Stone of Superbad *are friends, not competitors.*

For more information about Kellie's opening act during the *Fearless* tour, read Chapter 8.

Meet the Band

There's one group of friends who have always been prepared have Taylor's back: her band. Taylor's band is made up of seven talented musicians who help her music come to life: Caitlin Evanson, fiddle; Amos Heller, bass; Elizabeth Huett, backup vocals; Mike Meadows, banjo, mandolin, guitar, keyboards, cello; Grant Mickelson, guitar; Paul Sudoti, guitar; and Al Wilson, drums.

According to her fiddler, Caitlin,

say 'Well, can you kind of do this,' and she'll sing me a melody, and I'll incorporate that, and that's very impressive for someone her age," said Paul, who also praised Taylor's songwriting.

Taylor is equally enthralled with her band. She has both professional and personal relationships with each of them. When she doesn't see them for a while, she actually misses them. They do fun things together that have nothing to do with music, like playing basketball at Garth Brooks' house or watching *Grey's Anatomy* on the tour bus. They're a tight-knit group, with their own inside jokes. For example, the band started call-

got married, Taylor was beside herself with joy. "I couldn't be more happy that this will be the first wedding I've ever been to," she wrote on her MySpace blog. "I can't wait to bawl my eyes out and feel like love really means something and be all hopeful. Congratulations to Amos and Kara, who I love more than I can say."

The band has certainly been there for Taylor in sickness and in health. When Taylor got her wisdom teeth out, she was in bed for three days. "My band was amazing, they came over and sat with me, and we watched *CSI*," Taylor said of her healing process.

Taylor loves her band so much, she rewarded them—and their families—with a paid vacation to Hawaii. "They've all worked so hard for the past two years without a real break," she explained.

She wrote about the relaxing trip to Hawaii on her blog: "It's been the most AMAZING week and we all needed it," Taylor said. "It's so crazy to remember what it is to relax and not have plans. To wake up and think, 'What am I doing today?'...Oh yeah...NOTHING."

When they aren't vacationing in Hawaii, her band spends long hours on the road. Despite the hectic tour schedule, Taylor and her band always find time to connect before a show. Their nightly tradition is forming a motivational circle before heading onstage.

Sometimes they dance; other times they pray; and sometimes, they even say three little words to each other: I love you.

> ## Taylor is "a 40-year-old in a 19-year-old's body. She's made and meant to be doing what she's doing. She knows how to lead the room and lead the stage. And she knows how to do it too without being some taskmaster."

Taylor is "a 40-year-old in a 19-year-old's body. She's made and meant to be doing what she's doing. She knows how to lead the room and lead the stage. And she knows how to do it too without being some taskmaster."

Taylor's guitarist, Paul Sudoti, also respects the talent she demonstrates as a teenager. "There have been times where I've played a solo, and then she'll

ing themselves "The Agency" after shooting the video for "Picture to Burn." In the video, the band helps Taylor destroy her ex-boyfriend's house. "They got to dress up in suits and sunglasses and ransack a house," Taylor explained. "The scene of them walking across the yard in slow motion only encouraged this."

When her bass player, Amos Heller,

Taylor is good friends with her band; here she rocks with her guitarist Grant Mickelson.

Chapter Six

The Real Taylor Swift

Who is Taylor Swift, really? What does her house look like? What are her favorite things to do? What does she like to eat? Behind the glamourous designer dresses lies a "real" Taylor Swift—a girl who dips her French fries into her milkshakes, takes baths, and adores her snoring cat. She may be beautiful and famous, but deep down, Taylor Swift is an everyday girl.

At Home with the Swifts

Before buying her own condo in 2009 (see Chapter 8 for details about her new place), Taylor chose to live with her parents and her brother, Austin, in Hendersonville, Tennessee. At home, her family enjoys hanging out together in the kitchen, where Taylor likes to sit at the counter. They're a typical family in this way. Her brother talks about school, while her dad talks about stocks. Taylor likes being surrounded by the people she loves.

"They give me space, but I've still got people to talk to when I get lonely," said Taylor, whose good friends do not live in the Nashville area. "I'm afraid of what happens to people when they get lonely."

The Swift home is located on Old Hickory Lake in the green, rolling hills of Hendersonville, Tennessee. It's a large home but has a warm, cozy look. There are hardwood floors, formal rugs, and antiques, but also comfortable couches that Taylor described on MySpace. "I can't lie, they're some great couches," she wrote. "Giant, like you're lying on a bed. But it's not a bed. It's a couch. So you're all confused, but comfortable at the same time."

The house also features a music room filled with guitars and recording equipment. Taylor's awards and framed gold records are on display throughout the home. The sitting room used to house a rack of Taylor's dresses and outfits, items she needed to sort for Goodwill donations. Speaking of clothes, Taylor's closet is rather small for a country and pop superstar. However, it is very organized. At one time, she actually color-coded her clothes.

In October 2009, Taylor's fans got a sneak peek inside the star's house. Remember when Taylor surprised her ten-year-old fan Jordan on *The Oprah Winfrey Show*? That day, Oprah gave Jordan an important assignment: interview Taylor Swift during her *Fearless* tour. Jordan did her job, of course, and returned to *The Oprah Winfrey Show* to share her exclusive Taylor footage with the studio audience.

On Jordan's first day of being a journalist, she got a private tour of the Swift home. Jordan admitted to being nervous as her mom drove up the long driveway to Taylor's house, which sits back from the road, surrounded by a lush, green lawn and many trees.

Jordan climbed the many steps to Taylor's front door to meet her idol. Once inside the house, she saw the sitting room where Taylor wrote "Our Song." She also got a tour of Taylor's spacious, high-ceiling bedroom, where Taylor sleeps in a four-poster bed. From the posts, Taylor draped lavender and pink billowy scarves, which match her pink and purple comforter.

In the bedroom, Taylor pointed out a special spot to Jordan, "About five feet from us right there is the spot on the floor where I wrote 'Love Story,'" she told her fan "It's kind of funny for me to walk past it every day...that was a very productive 20 minutes."

Jordan also traveled inside Taylor's bathroom, where her idol showed her a pair of thick, black-framed glasses. "I'm pretty blind without glasses," Taylor admitted.

After the tour, Jordan interviewed Taylor, asking her questions about her childhood, adolescence, and boys. "Do you have a crush on anyone now?" Jordan asked.

Taylor said she did not currently have a boyfriend. "I'd rather be single than be with someone I kind of like, rather than really like," she explained.

The next day, Jordan went backstage and toured Taylor's bus. She ate lunch with Taylor's crew and even danced under the onstage waterfall Taylor uses during her concerts. That night, the ten-year-old stood in the front row of Taylor's concert.

"This is a dream come true," Jordan said at the end of the day, with many grateful tears. It was a dream come true for all of Taylor's fans; through Jordan, they learned more about the real Taylor Swift.

Home for the Holidays

Home is very important to Taylor, especially come Christmastime. Taylor doesn't tour during the holidays because she prefers to be home surrounded by loved ones. The Swift home is always very festive at that time of year; Taylor said Christmas decorating is her mom's sport. "My mom always goes crazy with the Christmas decorations and makes the house look like the North Pole," Taylor told *Girl's Life*. The Swifts have Christmas tree saltshakers, wreaths on every door, and garlands hanging off ledges.

On Christmas Eve, the Swifts usually go to church and then return home to open gifts. Taylor said her younger brother, Austin, acts like a little kid; he yells "presents" and runs around the house. Taylor also enjoys the holidays, but shopping for gifts always poses a problem. "I'm like an expert on talking myself out of buying something," she wrote on her MySpace blog. "So I take forever to shop for Christmas presents."

The Swifts have experienced a few troubles with Christmas dinner. One year, the oven broke, which compromised the preparation of their turkey.

Another year, they tried to cook the turkey in a deep fryer. "We had the little rig set up in the back yard with the big pot to fry the turkey in and the 50 barrels of oil," Taylor explained. "But when it came time to take the turkey out of the fryer, it was like...melted.... so needless to say, we had a vegetarian Christmas dinner that year."

These turkey mishaps might have ruined Christmas for some people, but Taylor didn't care. "See, I'd be perfectly content eating anything for Christmas dinner, it's Christmas," she said. "The food isn't what makes it awesome for me."

So what's on Taylor's Christmas wish list? Of course, she'd love any gift related to music. In fact, one of the best Christmas presents she ever received was an acoustic guitar—a one-of-a-kind dark blue one with fish swimming around the sound hole. She grabs that guitar when she wakes up with a song idea at 4 AM. Taylor loves that guitar, but her career and her fans mean the most to her. They are the best gifts she has received. "This Christmas is so much more special to me than any other, because I ultimately have already gotten what I wanted...this," Taylor wrote on her

Daddy's Little Girl

■ Because Taylor's father, Scott Swift, works full-time as a stockbroker, he cannot accompany Taylor on tour very often. But that doesn't mean the two aren't close. When he does tag along for a concert or event, he always brings his sense of humor along to brighten Taylor's day or sometimes, humiliate her.

"He's a social butterfly and loves being on tour. He loves it so much, he thinks it's absolutely hilarious to mess with me and try to embarrass me as much as possible," Taylor said of her dad.

For instance, when Taylor and her backup singer Liz walked into the quiet lobby of their hotel, they heard someone scream, "Hey! That's Taylor Swift!"

It wasn't a fan, though. "Dad. Please stop doing that," Taylor had to say.

Another time, at an award show, Taylor wore a dress made of small jewels and metal pieces. The small particles kept falling off of her dress. Her father followed close behind, and every time he picked a particle up off the floor, he said "eBay!" as if he planned to sell the remnants of her dress online.

Like most dads, Scott Swift worries about his daughter's image and public exposure. He keeps close tabs on what the media is saying about Taylor by receiving Google alerts. He's also concerned about her teeth. He once taped a note to the front seat of the airport car that read, "Taylor, don't forget your retainer. Dad."

Taylor's father, Scott Swift, brings humor on the road.

blog during the holidays. "People to care about my music, care about my lyrics, care about what I do, who I am."

Taylor also loves Christmas because of its close proximity to her birthday, December 13. Her birthday parties usually coincide with the holidays in theme. For her 19th birthday, her band and crew came to the house to celebrate. "Everyone was all dressed up, and the house was decorated for Christmas and everyone was so happy," she wrote on her blog. "We played all these games, one where each person gets to pick a present from under the tree, and you can choose to steal presents from other people. Then there was the ping-pong competition, which was pretty hardcore. We had a fire pit outside, and we made S'mores. It was a blast. Then almost everyone stayed really really late and jammed."

The year prior, for her 18th birthday, Tim McGraw and Faith Hill gave Taylor a pink Christmas tree, which she proudly displayed in her bedroom. She also received balloons from Reba McEntire and a Judith Leiber clutch from country singer John Rich, who co-wrote the song "The Way I Loved You" with Taylor. The biggest gift she received that year was a pink truck from her record label. Because Taylor already drove a car she loves—a champagne-colored Lexus SC 430 convertible, the same car featured in the film *Mean Girls*—she decided to donate the pink truck to Victory Junction, a camp for kids with chronic medical conditions.

Taylor felt good about the decision because she likes doing good deeds for others. "I love giving back to people because it's sort of like when you're looking forward to Christmas," she told *Cosmo Girl*. "Not because you're going to get presents, but because you've gotten your mom something really cool, and you can't wait to see her face when she opens it."

Lucky Number 13

■ Most people think the number 13 is unlucky, thanks to the infamous day of bad luck, Friday the 13th. But for Taylor Swift, the number 13 actually represents good luck. Taylor loves the number 13 so much, she has her mom paint it on her hand every night before she performs. It's a tradition. She also posts the number on her tour bus door.

So why is Taylor fascinated with the number 13? It all started with her birthday. "I was born on the 13th. I turned 13 on Friday the 13th. My first album went gold in 13 weeks. My first #1 song had a 13-second intro," she divulged. "Every time I've won an award I've been seated in either the 13th seat, the 13th row, the 13th section or row M, which is the 13th letter."

The coincidences get more interesting. Taylor's hit song "Love Story" went No. 1 in the 13th week of her album being out. That same week, her *Rolling Stone* cover hit newsstands. Furthermore, Taylor noticed her lucky number pop up in the episode of MTV's *Once Upon a Prom*, in which she made an appearance. Taylor's prom date, a boy named Whit, wore number 13 on his jersey while playing basketball. Later in the show, Whit said, "This is going to be cutting it close. I've got 13 minutes to get home."

Taylor credits her success to the support of her fans, but she still respects the power of her lucky number. "Basically whenever a 13 comes up in my life, it's a good thing," she said.

Indi, the Snoring Cat

When Taylor's back home in Hendersonville, she also spends time with her favorite furry friend, Indi. Apparently, the cat does not like anyone else in the family. When Taylor's gone, Indi throws temper tantrums. Taylor knows about Indi's antics because her father leaves her voicemails about the cat. "She's like the most miserable, depressed, whining cat ever when I'm not here," Taylor said. "She just wanders around the house screaming and howling."

Indi is known to make sounds besides purring. She actually snores. It's something Taylor writes about from time to time on her MySpace page. "I'm sitting on my bed, and my cat is sitting next to me SNORING so loudly.... And I'm trying not to laugh, because I'll wake her up....You just don't expect little cats to snore like that," she explained. "I tried to call Abigail so she could hear it, but she's off at college and is probably studying or doing something cooler than watching a cat snore."

Needless to say, Indi clings to Taylor, but the cat is not always happy when her owner is around. Taylor said the cat has "abandonment issues" and throws fits. The two have dramatic conversations together. "There's no reasoning with her when she's like this. Soon she'll be all 'Forgive me, I didn't mean it' and I'll be all 'How can I believe you?' and she'll be like 'I'm sorry' and I'll burst into song with 'You're NOT sorry. No, no, no-ohhhh,'" Taylor explained. When Taylor goes to sleep, Indi ceases the drama and follows her into bed. She curls up next to her and begins snoring. Sometimes, Indi snores and purrs at the same time, which is quite an interesting sound, according to Taylor.

Indi is not the only pet living with the Swift family. Taylor also owns two Doberman Pinschers, known to be aggressive dogs. "They're really sweet," Taylor told *CMT News*. "But if you break in, they will eat you."

Star-Struck

Taylor Swift knows what it's like to be a fan. She attended her first concert—LeAnn Rimes—when she was just eight years old and remembers the excitement of that night. Even though Taylor became a music star herself, she still gets star-struck when it comes to meeting her idols.

One of Taylor's most "pinch me" moments was meeting Shania Twain at the 2008 CMA Awards. The country and pop singer, who Taylor called "the most impressive and independent and confident and successful

Taylor took the staff of Blender *magazine out for lunch at the Hendersonville Applebee's.*

Good Eats

■ When it comes to dining, Taylor is very informal. For example, while being interviewed for *Blender*, she took the magazine staff out to lunch at the local Applebee's in Hendersonville. When chatting with *Rolling Stone* magazine, she baked mocha chocolate-chip cookies. Another time, while shooting the cover photos for *Cosmo Girl*, she munched on a Nathan's hot dog with extra ketchup.

So does she eat her veggies? Not very often. In fact, she hates healthy foods like vegetables and sushi. But she does love to bake, and treats it like a science, measuring everything just so.

Below is a list of Taylor's other favorite things to eat.

Favorite Restaurant: Cracker Barrel for scrambled eggs, sausage patties, and biscuits with apple butter; "It's where I go when I'm on the road and want to be reminded of home," she said.

Favorite Drink: The virgin piña coladas at the Four Seasons Hualalai Resort in Kona, Hawaii.

Favorite Candy: Watermelon Sour Patch Kids; she can't live without them!

Favorite Coffee: Starbuck's—if she doesn't have coffee in the morning, she gets a headache at night.

Favorite Salad Dressing: Raspberry-walnut vinaigrette; she carries this grocery store find around with her.

Favorite L.A. Eatery: In-N-Out Burger; she even dips her fries into her chocolate shake.

Favorite Vitamins: Flintstone's Sour Gummies Vitamins; her mom had to confiscate them because she ate too many.

"It's just so wonderful when you're a fan of someone, you picture them as a sincere, genuine person, and they prove you right."

female artist to ever hit country music," is one of the reasons Taylor wanted to become a singer.

"She walked up to me and said she wanted to meet me and tell me I was doing a great job," Taylor wrote on her MySpace blog. "She was so beautiful, guys. She really IS that beautiful. All the while, I was completely star-struck. After she walked away, I realized I didn't have my camera. Then I cried."

Taylor has met famous television and movie stars as well. Once, while playing at a corporate party, Taylor and her band got to meet actress Keri Russell, who starred in the television show *Felicity* and the movie *The Waitress*. Taylor said she is obsessed with Keri because "she rocks the curly hair." Meeting Keri was a great experience for Taylor because the actress was so down to earth. That night, Taylor's banjo player at the time, Ben, asked Keri how she styles her hair because his wife wanted to know. Believe it or not, Keri told him. "This is why she's awesome: she gets out a piece of paper, and writes down EXACTLY what products she uses, what blow dryers she uses, and exactly what she does to make her hair straight or curly," Taylor said. "It seems simple, but she had so many people who wanted to talk to her, and still she took the time to do that for Ben. I just think it's so awesome when cool people don't know they're cool."

Taylor got the opportunity to meet several of her favorite stars when she co-hosted MTV's *Total Request Live (TRL)*. There, she met Anne Hathaway, another actress she admires. "I loved her in *Becoming Jane* and *The Devil Wears Prada*," explained Taylor. "I've always looked up to her for how

she carries herself with class." Taylor also met *The Office* star Steve Carell, who she said was "hilarious and sweet." Anne and Steve were at *TRL* promoting the film *Get Smart*.

For Taylor, the highlight of being on *TRL* was getting to chat with R & B singer Rihanna. "She's amazing and gorgeous and SO cool to talk to," Taylor said. "A lot of the time, superstars have huge entourages around them, and it's really intimidating and weird. But Rihanna had one, maybe two people with her. It was so cool to see that. We talked backstage during commercial breaks, and she was real and outgoing and funny."

Another person Taylor admires is Richard Curtis, the writer and director of her favorite movie, *Love Actually*. "I've been a fan of everything he's done," Taylor explained. "I think he's one of the only people who is possibly as obsessed with the concept of love as I am." Turns out, Richard Curtis brought his wife and kids to see Taylor Swift in concert in May 2009. They came backstage after the show to say hello and chat. The next day, Richard sent a box of gifts to Taylor's hotel room. Inside was a signed copy of the *Love Actually* screenplay, DVDs of Richard's other films, and a heartfelt letter. "It's just so wonderful when you're a fan of someone, you picture them as a sincere, genuine person, and they prove you right," Taylor said. "I love it when that happens."

Speaking of gifts from celebrities, Taylor once received a gift that made her cry. While playing a concert in Bakersville, California, the son of the late country legend Buck Owens gave her a red, white, and blue guitar. "Buck used to give them to (musicians) that he really respected, and

(his son) said that this was the first one they had given away since we lost Buck," Taylor explained to the *Reading Eagle*. "It blew my mind. I got really, really emotional. It was just so different than any other sort of respect. It was being approved and embraced by a country legend."

Of all Taylor's meet-and-greets with stars, her meeting with Def Leppard was the most documented. Taylor and her mom are big fans of the band known for hits like "Pour Some Sugar on Me" and "Photograph." Taylor got to perform with Def Leppard for an episode of CMT *Crossroads*. Of course, her mom accompanied her to the filming.

"She was so star-struck, and so was my entire band and I, because before we go onstage we all listen to Def Leppard music and jump around and get ready," Taylor explained. "(We) were just looking at each other like, 'This is not happening, you've got to be kidding me.'"

Taylor wasn't shy around her favorite band. She brought a digital camera with her and asked her mom to record the event. "I was like, 'Mom, please don't miss any of this,'" Taylor said.

Even though they have sold over 60 million records, the band members of Def Leppard were very easy-going, which surprised Taylor. "I thought that they would be divas. I thought that they would be snobby. I thought that they would only want to sing certain things and would only let me sing certain things," she said. "When I walked in, I very timidly and politely asked Joe Elliott (the lead singer) if I could sing one of the lines in 'Hysteria.' He goes, 'Honey I've been singing that for 25 years—you sing whatever you want.'"

Not every meet-and-greet with an idol has been one hundred percent positive. Taylor has had her share of embarrassing moments. While performing in San Antonio, Taylor noticed her fiddler, Caitlin, was wearing unique leggings under her skirt. They were silver and reflective. Sometimes, Taylor and her band members tease each other about clothes, so it was only natural for Taylor to yell, "Caitlin looks like a space stripper!" before heading into her dressing room.

It was a comment she soon regretted, though. "I turn the corner, and standing in my dressing room is.... George Strait and his wife, Norma. I literally was so mortified, I fell to the floor and my face was BRIGHT red," Taylor explained. "We all burst out laughing and hung out for about an hour. I don't think anything has ever surprised me as much, and I honestly never thought I'd get to say that George Strait came to watch one of my shows."

So, of all the stars Taylor admires, who did she say she'd trade places with for the day? Hayley Williams from Paramore. "I think she's awesome, and their music is amazing," Taylor said.

If she was stuck in an elevator, however, Taylor would choose a more humorous companion, like Ellen DeGeneres. "That situation would panic a lot of people, but she'd be like, 'Hey, whatever!' and make a joke," Taylor said of the talk show comedian. "Then we'd laugh and dance."

Musical Tastes

Obviously, Taylor loves music. But she doesn't sit around listening to her own tunes. She loves many other types of music besides country, especially hip-hop. "I feel like country and hip-hop are two of the most honest genres because we just like to sing about our lifestyle," she said. "We like to sing about the things that go on in our daily activities, and we're proud of the way we live, and we're proud of the things that we stand for."

What Taylor most appreciates about hip-hop is its rhyming. Lyrics, in essence, are poetry, something Taylor wrote before she started writing songs. "I found out that if you get the right amount of words and the right syncopation, and you get the right rhymes at the end, you can make words bounce off of a page," said Taylor, who enjoys the music of Eminem and even covers his song "Lose Yourself" during her concerts. "So hip-hop has always been something that I looked at and thought, 'Wow, that really is an incredible art form.'"

Eminem happens to be one of the artists on Taylor's iPod, which is full of an eclectic mix of tunes. "My iPod

Taylor, the Paparazzi

■ It's not surprising Taylor recorded her meeting with Def Leppard. She's known for making video blogs for her MySpace page. "A lot of the time, if I'm at an event with other celebrities, I want to get it on film," she said." I'm like the biggest super-fan there."

Taylor uses her obsession with other stars to her advantage, though. She discovered it's a great way to promote her own work. Before her *Fearless* album came out, she brought her digital camera to the CMT Awards. "I have Hank Williams Jr., Brad Paisley, George Jones, George Strait, Miranda Lambert, Martina McBride, and Dierks Bently. All the artists I love were there, and I got them all to say, 'Taylor's album comes out November 11—go get it,'" She explained. "I was so paparazzi, it's not even funny."

That's right, Taylor has no shame when it comes to marketing herself and her music. She actually downloaded her own music on iTunes to change its rank position. She wanted a song to hit the top ten, so she bought it herself. "When it was sitting at 11, I downloaded it. And it went into the top 10. Then I really wanted it to be top five, so I downloaded it again when it was sitting at six. Then I really wanted it to be No. 1 when my album came out, so I downloaded it again, and then it went No. 1."

She also admitted another act of self-promotion. "My newest hobby is going to Walmart and putting my CD in front of others in the rack," she said. "I have no shame in it!"

is full of everything: Ingrid Michaelson, Matt Carney, the Dixie Chicks, Rascal Flatts...and then I have Kanye West and Eminem," she explained. "My musical taste is all over the place."

That's true, because she also listens to Boys Like Girls, Faith Hill, Heidi Newfield, Hellogoodbye, Jonas Brothers, Katy Perry, Kings of Leon, and Metro Station. Furthermore, Taylor's cell phone ringtones include "Taylor" by Jack Johnson, "It's Over" by Jesse McCartney, and "You're so Vain" by Carly Simon. In this way, Taylor's musical tastes span decades. One of her favorite songs is the 1990 cover song "Nothing Compares to You" by Sinead O'Connor. It's a song Taylor sometimes puts on repeat play.

"I discovered it last year, and I feel like there's a timeless thing that that song has," Taylor said of Sinead's hit tune, which was actually written by Prince. "It's just one of those songs where you know that when it was written, like 5,000 songwriters just put their pen down and went, 'Alright. I tried'...I think it's a brilliant song."

Down Time

Listening to music and making playlists is something Taylor does in her free time. She likes to read too. Her favorite book in school was *To Kill a Mockingbird* by Harper Lee because she said, "I'm very interested in any writing from a child's perspective."

She also enjoys painting. "I'm interested in Jackson Pollock's kind of art, where art is beautiful but it's nothing and yet it's incredible," she said. Once, she created a few pieces in Jackson Pollack's style—paint

Taylor's **Music Q & A**

What are Taylor's favorite lyrics?
"Something written by one of my favorite radio guys, who is also a songwriter: 'If there was no change, there would be no butterflies.' He once sent me a thank-you note and quoted that at the bottom, writing, 'I'm sure everyone is telling you don't change. But I think the right thing to say is to always embrace change gracefully.'"

According to Taylor, what is the funniest country song?
"'She Thinks My Tractor's Sexy' has got to take the cake on that one!" she said.

If Taylor could listen to only one album on a cross-country drive, what would it be?
Def Leppard, *Pyromania*

What type of music does Taylor wish she knew more about?
"Hair metal. I've always been so focused on Def Leppard that I never explored other metal bands," Taylor said. "That's what my band talks about, and I can't keep up.

splattered on a canvas in a random pattern—which she sent as gifts to the managers of country music radio stations. When she paints, she likes to light candles and listen to music. It's relaxing. Taylor also likes to go to the grocery store. Writing letters is another favorite pastime.

She doesn't play sports often and admitted she doesn't run very fast. She is good at trivia games, especially questions about pop culture. She's a big fan of movies, television, and celebrities. Her favorite movie is *Love Actually*—she can say all the lines in a British accent. "It's one of

those movies with an amazing ending that makes you want a boyfriend on Christmas," said Taylor. "Because of that, I can only watch it once a year."

Her favorite television show is *CSI*, especially *CSI: Las Vegas*. She also loves the situational humor on *Grey's Anatomy*. She can't always watch episodes when they air, so she catches up by watching them on DVD. She said she watches *Grey's Anatomy* when she feels stressed or lonely, and she watches them more than once. She refers to it as "her show" and even downloads all the songs played on the show. Her favorite character was Izzie's boyfriend, Denny Duquette, who died in Season 3. Taylor cried for days after that happened. "It was borderline embarrassing," she said.

When she's not blogging on MySpace, Taylor likes to read other blogs; her favorites are Ocean Up, Just Jared, and Paris Hilton.

Taylor's life when she's not on the road may sound boring compared to the lives of other 19-year-olds. People often ask her, "Don't you want to rebel?" When it comes to life, Taylor doesn't need to go out and party to be happy. "Rebellion is what you make of it," she told *Rolling Stone*. "When you've been on a tour bus for two months straight, and then you get in your car and drive wherever you want, that can feel rebellious."

Taylor said she rebels in other ways, by writing honest songs and naming real people in her lyrics. "To me, rebelling is—is that rush you get when you sing a song about someone and you know they're in the crowd," she told *Dateline NBC*. "Like, that's a really fun rebellion for me."

The Talented Taylor Swift

There's no doubt Taylor is talented musically, but what would she be doing if she hadn't gone into music? If she went to college, Taylor said she would not major in music. "When music becomes technical for me, I don't like that part of it," she said. "When you're reading music, for me, it turns into math. I like for it to go the way it's going to go. I'm not as much into technique as I am into the emotion of it."

Her mother believes she would have been a writer. "If music hadn't worked out, I think she'd be going off to college to take journalism classes or trying to become a novelist," Andrea Swift told *The Washington Post*. "But her writing took an interesting twist when she picked up the guitar and applied her writing to music."

Police work is another possible, alternative career for Taylor. "I would be in some sort of criminal investigation process, Homeland Security or something like that," she said. On the other hand, she might have gone into business development and advertising. "Sometimes, I think of ideas for products," Taylor explained. "How about a van company called Van Go?"

Taylor does have a few surprising skills. In addition to playing guitar, she also plays the piano and the ukulele, which she learned in Hawaii. Perhaps her most unique talent is her ability to take pictures with one hand.

"I realized that I have very long arms, so I can take the perfect arm-length picture with fans," she said. "I can take the perfect MySpace pictures."

Bad Luck: Nightmares and More

■ Taylor may have a lucky number, but she sometimes thinks negative thoughts. One thing she deals with often is nightmares. "I have a recurring dream that people are lined up next to my bed, waiting for autographs and taking pictures of me," Taylor said.

Other dreams are more serious. In one, Taylor was chased by a girl. "I was like, I don't want your boyfriend! It was a couple I know, and I like both of them. I can't even remember everything that was going on but I was like, running," Taylor explained. "That's my biggest fear. Getting in trouble for something I didn't do."

This fear has prompted another dream. In it, Taylor was accused of a crime she didn't commit. "The police are coming after me with handcuffs and my mom is crying and asking where she went wrong," Taylor told *Seventeen*. "I'm screaming 'I didn't do it!' but no one can hear me."

Bad things have happened to Taylor in real life as well. Below is a list of Taylor's run-ins with bad luck.

Car Accidents: "I've been in three accidents, but none of them were my fault," she divulged to *Rolling Stone*.
Lost Documents: While traveling in Germany, Taylor lost her passport.
Rumors: There was a rumor circulating that Taylor was pregnant. Taylor called the rumor "the most IMPOSSIBLE thing on the planet."
Hackers: Taylor's MySpace account has been compromised by computer hackers. "I just love it when they hack in and delete my pictures and change my top friends and wreak other various forms of havoc," she said. "Not."

Chapter Seven

A "Taylored" Look

Taylor Swift was not born with her fashion sense; it's something she discovered over time. As a kid, she wore mock turtlenecks with zippers, which were in style in the 1990s. As a young teen, she once wore a black bra under a see-through shirt, but that look—possibly inspired by Britney Spears—didn't stick. Most days, she wore faded jeans and sneakers, but in the early part of her country music career, she started wearing cowboy hats, studded belts and even handkerchief-hemmed dresses. Eventually, she found a style all her own.

From red carpet gowns to sundresses, from high heels to cowboy boots, Taylor Swift embraces a unique fashion sense. Sometimes her look is sophisticated; other times, it's edgy and urban. Then, she has those moments of pure country. It seems Taylor Swift is "fearless" when it comes to fashion. She dresses according to the event she's attending or her mood. And she's not afraid to mix and match styles to create a one-of-a-kind look.

The Red Carpet

As a country and pop music superstar, Taylor has attended dozens of award shows, where trendy red carpet dresses and gowns are a must. At these events, fashion seems to be as important as the awards themselves. For this reason, Taylor loves to attend awards shows. "I get so excited about these things because I love to dress up," she said.

Taylor started out her award show wardrobe at the 2007 Academy of Country Music (ACM) Awards, where she wore a long, light pink ball gown. The top was fitted and covered in sequins, while the tulle skirt flowed around her. She was only 17 years old,

but she looked sophisticated on the night she first met country singer Tim McGraw.

Later that year, Taylor wore her "favorite dress ever" to the Country Music Awards (CMAs), where she won the coveted Horizon Award. She looked like a princess in the light gold dress, which boasted a snug, shimmer bodice and a full shirt made of layered satin. The dress was designed by Taylor's personal stylist, Sandi Spika Borchetta, the vice president of Big Machine Records and also Scott's wife. Later that night, Taylor totally changed her look. She performed in a small black dress, accessorized by gloves she altered for the performance. "I cut holes in the fingers of these long, black gloves so I could play guitar," she told *Allure*.

One of Taylor's trends, when it comes to formal dresses, is shimmer. She often wears silver or gold dresses that sparkle in some way or another. The first time she attended the BMI Country Awards, she wore a black cocktail dress covered in jewels. One of her other favorite sparkly dresses is the Kaufman Franco piece she wore to the 2008 CMAs. It was made of jewels, platinum chips, and other metal pieces. "My red carpet dress weighed about 400 pounds. Actually, about 30. But it was still heavy," Taylor explained. "It was like dragging around two small children, dangling from my ankles. And it made a lovely jangling noise whenever I walked.... Whenever people would ask me what it was made of, I'd just say I broke a mirror, dipped myself in glue, and rolled around in it."

This sparkly dress actually fell apart during the night. The metal pieces came off, and Taylor's dad

picked them up, joking he'd sell them on eBay. Despite all the trouble, Taylor was happy with her choice. "This dress took more effort than any big dress I've ever worn, and you know how I like big dresses," she said. "But it was well worth it, because it was my favorite dress I've ever worn...and I was lucky to get to wear it."

Another infamous sparkly dress is the one Taylor wore to the 2009 MTV Video Music Awards. Because of the Kanye West incident—he interrupted her on stage—the dress was photographed more than it might have been. It was a sheer fabric dress, covered in silver rhinestones. It draped over one shoulder—a look she has worn many times before— and showed off a good portion of her back. It completed the princess look she was going for that night; she'd arrived at the VMAs in a horse-drawn carriage driven by a man wearing a cowboy hat. "I have a castle complex," Taylor said about her arrival. "I love fairytales." Later that night, when Taylor sang "You Belong With Me," she changed into a vintage, short red dress and Christian Louboutin pumps. This is actually the dress she wore when she gave her acceptance speech; she had already changed into it when Beyonce called her back onstage.

Sometimes Taylor finds subtle ways to sparkle. For example, when she attended the premiere of the Zach Efron film *17 Again* in Sydney, Australia, she wore a plain, long white dress. Rhinestones covered the neckline, however, and gave the simple dress a touch of bling. Other times, Taylor replaces sparkle with color. She wore a vibrant lilac, floor-sweeping gown to the 2008 Grammys and a berry colored V-neck dress to the 2008 CMT Music Awards.

When choosing dresses for events, Taylor considers many things, but in the end, she is quite practical. "As far as a look, I try to dress for weather," she said. "As far as places, I only really factor in what I should wear differently in a different city if there's a weather change." In cities like Los Angeles, she's free to wear short skirts and strapless gowns. But when the weather is chilly, Taylor does not trade warmth for glamour. When she attended the Rockefeller Center Christmas Tree Lighting Ceremony, she wore a black turtleneck under an ankle-length cream coat.

Taylor may be practical, but she also appreciates fashion risks. She looks to her music idols for ideas on what to wear to events. "I like when people really experiment with color," said Taylor, noting how much she admires the style of R&B singer Rihanna. "Everything that she has decided to wear as far as fashion on the carpet [has always looked good]. She takes chances... it's all about color and

Taylor the **Fashion Correspondent**

■ In 2008, Taylor Swift served as the MTV fashion correspondent for the Video Music Awards. It was a very special honor for Taylor. "...For the hour before the awards start, I'll be interviewing all the artists and celebrities on the red carpet! SO excited," she wrote on her MySpace blog. "There's no way I thought I was going to get to be here tonight."

Taylor, who was nominated for Best New Artist that year, wore two dresses to the event. First, she wore a nude colored Kaufman Franco dress, which boasted a smooth bodice and a flared skirt. Her colorful open-toed shoes were designed by Giuseppe Zanotti. When reporters asked how she'd prepared for the evening, she told them she'd eaten at In–N–Out Burger earlier that day. The burger joint is "necessary for all red carpets in L.A." according to Taylor.

"I had one person doing my hair, and one person doing my make-up, and then I got dressed," she added. "Low key day, actually."

When it came time to interview stars, Taylor changed into a short, shiny gold dress decorated with embroidery and gemstones. She really sparkled while interviewing music sensations like Pink and Katy Perry. For Taylor, the fashion correspondent position required a good amount of acting. She also had to interview the Jonas Brothers that night, and she was secretly dating Joe Jonas at the time. Taylor acted very professional around Joe, except when they hugged. During their embrace, she seemed to smell his hair.

The following year, Ashley Greene of the *Twilight* films took on the job of fashion correspondent at the MTV VMAs. Of course, Taylor shared a few words of wisdom with Ashley. She said a good correspondent must be able to think on her feet. "You never know who's going to walk up," Taylor said.

being risky."

Although Taylor has worn Kaufman Franco dresses, as well as those designed by personal stylist Sandi Spika Borchetta, she would like to wear pieces by other well-known designers. Her taste in red carpet fashion continues to evolve. "I've learned a lot. I go to all these photo shoots, and each time I figure out something new about myself and what I want to wear,"

"I felt so much like I was in high school again—in a good way, without any drama, without anyone being catty."

Taylor said. "For a big night, I like Marchesa or Badgley Mischka—and I love Oscar de la Renta. I've never gotten to wear one of his dresses; if I ever did, I would probably faint."

Once upon a Prom

For the average teenage girl, there are few dress-up moments more exciting than prom. Taylor Swift has actually attended three of them. Her first prom experience took place her freshman year of high school. Her boyfriend, Drew, was a senior at the time and he took her as his date.

Another year, Taylor went with a boy named Cody. It was a last-minute invitation from a friend, and Taylor said yes. "I'll never forget getting asked to go to prom two days before, buying a $40 dress, and having the time of my life," she explained. Photos of Cody and Taylor from that night reveal a color-coordinated couple. Taylor wore a white dress, while Cody wore a white tuxedo with white vest and tie.

Taylor's third and most memorable prom didn't take place at her own school. In April 2008, Taylor attended the Hillcrest High School prom in Tuscaloosa, Alabama, for an episode of MTV's *Once Upon a Prom*, which aired in June of that year.

About 14 boys without prom dates competed for a date with a celebrity.

None of the boys knew Taylor Swift was the celebrity when they filmed their audition video. Taylor's options included a set of twins promising a "two for one" night of fun, a boy who had just broken up with his girl-friend, and a videogame enthusiast. After watching the video with her best friend, Abigail, Taylor couldn't decide which boy she should take to the prom. Upon Abigail's suggestion, Taylor put all the names on slips of paper inside a hat, and Abigail picked the winner. The lucky boy was Whit Wright, the only boy on the video to mention his specific admiration of Taylor Swift.

Whit, a baseball player who had just moved to Tuscaloosa the year before, found out the exciting news during an all school assembly at Hillcrest High School. After his name was announced, Whit received many congratulations. Fellow male students immediately approached him to "save a dance" with Taylor. The news was so mind-blowing, Whit had difficulty concentrating in class the rest of the school day.

On the big day, Whit waited outside his house for Taylor's tour bus to arrive. He wore a black tuxedo with a pink vest and tie, and he held a bouquet of flowers for his date. "Is he standing out there with flowers?" Taylor said from her tour bus. "That's

the cutest thing I've ever seen."

Taylor, who wore a BCBG long, beige dress with sparkly bodice, went inside Whit's house to take pictures with his family. There, he also gave her a corsage. When they left, the tour bus drove through the neighbor-hood, which was full of Taylor fans waving at the bus from the sidewalk.

Before prom, the couple joined the other seniors for a boat ride and dinner on the *Bama Belle*. On the boat, Taylor Swift proved she was an ordinary girl. In the buffet line, Taylor's plate slipped, and her food fell off. "That's awesome," she said, unfazed by the accident. After she ate, Whit noticed Taylor went back up to the buffet for seconds. "That's my kind of girl," he said of his hungry date.

On the boat, Taylor took a lot of pictures with Hillcrest High School students. She also found a date for her best friend. Whit's friend, Wayne, also did not have a date, so they paired him up with Abigail.

"I haven't hung out with people my age for like three years," Taylor ex-claimed on the boat. "This is so cool; I'm having so much fun."

After the boat ride, Taylor and Whit rode to the dance in her tour bus. It was then she learned why her date chose a pink vest and tie. Whit told Taylor that his friend's mother—a woman nicknamed "Aunt Joan," who is like a second mom to him—had been diagnosed with breast cancer. He wore pink that night to support her and the cause. After hearing this, Taylor excused herself from the group and returned wearing a short, light pink dress by designer Sue Wong, something she had in her closet on the bus. Taylor told Whit she wanted to support Aunt Joan, too.

The theme of the evening was "A Night in the Spotlight," and the Hillcrest High School prom committee transformed the school stairway into a red carpet. Soon, the pink-themed couple descended the steps while the crowd below watched. Taylor held on tightly to Whit's arm because she didn't want to fall

Throughout the dance, Taylor recognized guys from the audition video; she made a point to talk to each boy and mention the unique traits she remembered about him. Many of the students wore glow-in-the-dark necklaces that night, and Taylor did too. She admitted she wasn't good at

fast dancing, but she did slow dance with Whit to the duet "It's Your Love" by Tim McGraw and Faith Hill.

"I felt so much like I was in high school again—in a good way, without any drama, without anyone being catty," said Taylor, who would not attend her own prom that year due to her tour schedule. "It was the coolest thing!"

At the end of the night, Taylor opted out of post prom. After all, she had to ride the tour bus back to Nashville. She hugged Whit goodbye outside of the school; no kissing, because she doesn't kiss on first dates. But that doesn't mean she didn't think highly of Whit. "This guy was so down to earth and all-

American," she said of her prom date. "He was unbelievably sweet."

Whit was also happy with how the night went. "She acted toward me like I was one of her best friends, and I really liked that," he said. "She was everything I imagined and more."

Taylor likes proms so much, she chose "prom" as the theme for her "Our Song" No. 1 party. For the occasion, Taylor wore a light gray corset-top dress with a flared tulle skirt. She also wore a tiara with the words "Our Song" spelled out in rhinestones.

After attending three different proms, Taylor shared her experiences with *Your Prom* magazine; she was fea-

Trash to **Treasure**

■ A prom dress is not a practical purchase. A girl usually wears the expensive dress only once. What do you do with a used prom dress? If you're Taylor Swift, you donate it to a good cause.

Taylor donated a gold-and-cream Jessica McClintock dress to an organization that provides dresses for girls who can't afford them. "I chose to give away this prom dress because I wore it once and loved it," Taylor told *People* magazine. "To keep it around, hanging there all by itself and lonely in my closet, never to be worn again seemed a little pointless. I want another girl somewhere to feel good in it and have a great prom night because of this dress."

The dress was not given away, but put on auction, where it made $1, 200. The auction took place on donatemydress.org, a website that offers a national directory of dress drive locations.

Taylor encourages other girls to follow her example and donate their used prom dresses to a local dress drive. You can search donatemydress.org for a nearby location.

Joan Jett was Taylor's inspiration for a disco party during CRS week. Taylor dressed up like the rocker to sing "I Love Rock-n-Roll."

Playing **Dress Up**

■ Like her mom, who dressed up as a nerdy chaperone for Taylor's prom-themed "Our Song" No. 1 party, Taylor also enjoys wearing costumes. During Country Radio Seminar Week in March 2008, Taylor attended a disco party put on by radio personality Blair Garner of *After Midnite with Blair Garner*, something she'd never attended before. "Everyone dresses up in 70s attire and the artists sing 70s covers. The more you get into it, the better," Taylor explained on her MySpace blog.

Taylor certainly got into it. She sang "I Love Rock-n-Roll" by Joan Jett and wore a full costume, including a "brown wig and leather pants and a purple slasher guitar."

Taylor also dressed up for Halloween in 2006. She wore an angel costume with large wings during a performance. "That really conflicted with my guitar playing," she said of the wings. To elaborate on her costume, she asked her guitar players at the time, Todd and Kevin, to wear red, pointy devil ears.

In August 2009, Taylor wore a "surprising" costume when she pranked Keith Urban during a Kansas City concert performance of his song "Kiss a Girl." Shortly after Keith started playing, Taylor and her band came on stage looking like the members of the band Kiss. Taylor dressed like "Spaceman" from the band; she wore a black wig, white face make up, and silver and black bursts around her eyes. She even interrupted Keith to sing a few lines from his song.

tured on the cover of the spring 2009 issue. In the article, Taylor admitted she's "addicted to proms" but she also gave some good advice to prom-goers. "Be a social butterfly," she said. "Don't just hang with your boyfriend. Save the slow dances for him, but dance with everyone. And don't let petty prom drama ruin the evening."

Casually Cool

When Taylor is not going to fancy occasions like an award show or prom, she usually opts for a casual look. In fact, her favorite T-shirt has the periodic table printed on the front. Her other favorites include sundresses from French Connection, J. Crew blazers, and Victoria's Secret bikinis.

Taylor also wears jeans, shirtdresses, and white button-down shirts, which she sometimes tucks into a flared floral skirt. Other times, she takes her casual look up a notch. For an appearance on the *Late Show with David Letterman*, she wore a short, high-waist pouf skirt with a black turtleneck, black patterned tights, and black knee-high boots. The overall look was casual but very chic.

Although Taylor shops for everyday clothes at expensive stores like BCBG, she also loves to buy outfit essentials at less expensive stores. Her favorite fashion buy is "cheap clothing that looks like it's not cheap from Forever 21 or Walmart," she said.

For example, Taylor arrived at a cover shoot for *Cosmo Girl* magazine wearing blue gym shorts, a yellow T-shirt from Forever 21, brown-fringed suede boots, and braided bracelets. "I love my $20 outfit," she told the magazine staff that day.

Taylor knows price is a factor for most people when purchasing clothes;

that's why she was so excited about her exclusive line of L.E.I. dresses available at Walmart. The sundresses are affordable—about $14—and offer girls the opportunity to look like Taylor Swift. After all, her favorite casual look is a sundress and cowboy boots; it's the perfect balance between dressed up and dressed down. She started pairing boots with dresses when she performed at rodeos, and she still embraces the look today. It's what she wore to MTV Studios for co-hosting *Total Request Live*.

Because she toured during the summer, sundresses became a necessity in her closet, and they inspired her L.E.I. line. Taylor's favorite dress from the line is a cap-sleeve, open-back empire waist dress. When Taylor hosted a preview party for her new clothing line, she wore this very dress in black and accessorized her look with a cardigan and a pendant necklace. The dresses come in many different colors and styles.

Of course, the dresses all pair well with cowboy boots. Although Taylor wears both cowboy boots and high heels, it seems boots are her shoe of choice. Her height has something to do with that. "I'm 5'11", so when I wear heels, it's definitely a really good view that I have," she told *Entertainment Weekly*. "I'm like 6' 2" when I wear heels, so I tend to wear cowboy boots a lot."

Boots are easier to walk in and offer stability. "I wear cowboy boots so that when I walk down the stairs, I won't fall," Taylor explained. "I have this fear of falling in front of large groups of people. That's why I tend not to wear heels."

Unlike cowboy boots, high heels have caused Taylor major pain in

"I'm 5'11", so when I wear heels, it's definitely a really good view that I have..."

the past. She wore heels to the CMA Awards, and her feet were "killing" her before she even got to her designated spot. "I was hobbling up the aisle to my seat," Taylor said. "It was not ladylike."

That night, Taylor shared her foot pain with country singer Faith Hill, who offered a solution. "Take them off," Faith said.

"I was like, well, Faith Hill told me to, so I took off my shoes and carried them in my hand," Taylor explained. "She taught me that I don't have to take everything so seriously."

Taylor ended up presenting the award for Breakthrough Video of the Year in bare feet.

The Finishing Touch

A dress or great pair of jeans is only one part of the fashion equation. The other part is accessories, which give an outfit a finished look. Taylor loves to accessorize, especially with jewelry.

When it comes to jewelry, Taylor is obsessed with bracelets. She rarely wears just one, and she only wears them on her left wrist because she needs her right hand to strum the guitar. She often pairs a sparkly dress with long, dangling earrings, but tries to keep her look simple. For example, Taylor will pair a bejeweled dress with less eye-catching jewelry, like hoop earrings.

Taylor also uses accessories to add color to a look. She once wore a simple, floral sundress but added

color with turquoise flats and purple sunglasses. Another great accessory is a jacket. Taylor is known to add glamour to her look by wearing an Audrey Hepburn-inspired button up coat. Her biggest splurge on an accessory was a pair of Christian Louboutin heeled boots she wears all winter long.

One accessory Taylor rarely wears is her glasses, because she usually wears contacts. They are black frame and look a lot like the ones she wore in the video "You Belong With Me." She chose those frames because she felt sorry for them. She knew if she didn't buy them, no one else would.

Taylor also loves ban.do headbands; they come in many different colors and styles. Some even have gemstones or flowers attached. Taylor often wears them "hippie-style" across her forehead. The headbands bring a touch of whimsy to any outfit.

Another way to finish a look is through cosmetics. When it comes to make up, Taylor's "can't live without" item is black eyeliner. She uses it to define her eyes, which she emphasizes with smoky hues. For her eyelashes, she likes Chanel Inimitable Mascara. When she dramatizes her eyes, she opts for a more subdued color on her lips and cheeks. This way, she lets one feature take center stage. On tour, Taylor uses MAC body paint to draw stars and hearts on her face. She also has a signature scent. She wears Estée Lauder Bronze Goddess.

In the **Bag**

■ Like most women, Taylor Swift carries a purse to keep all of her goodies nearby. No matter the color or style, Taylor's purse must be big enough to carry her "must have" items. These include "a black Juicy Couture wallet from my first boyfriend, my iPhone, two iPods, Mace, and a key chain that looks like a cat but is really a knife," said Taylor.

She also carries her diary around with her, which makes her purse heavy. "My purse weighs, like, 50 pounds because my diary's in there and it weighs so much—it's the thickness of a Bible!" she told *Seventeen*. "I always have to have a diary or a journal with me wherever I go because I'm constantly writing stuff down, whether it's what happened to me that day, or an idea for a song in the middle of the night."

"It's very tropical," Taylor said.

Taylor admitted to committing one cosmetic no-no: She doesn't always wash her face at the end of the day. "I'm really lazy and sometimes I have my make up on for three days straight," she divulged.

There's one accessory Taylor Swift never goes without: her guitar. It's the one thing that always complements her outfit. Her guitars seem to match not only the song, but also her dress or the mood of a performance.

Taylor's technicians even gave her guitar nicknames: Sparkles, Koa, and Black Electric. "Sparkles" is covered in crystals and looks awesome up against a black dress, as in the video for "Our Song." The Koa acoustic guitar—made of high quality Koa wood from Hawaii—has a natural look to it.

On the other hand, her black electric guitar offers a clean, sleek style.

All of Taylor Swift's guitars are Taylor Guitars, as in guitars designed by legendary guitar maker Bob Taylor. Many other musicians use Taylor Guitars, including George Strait, Lee Ann Womack, and even Shakira.

Healthy Body Image

The media photograph Taylor often, whether she wears a ball gown or jeans and a T-shirt. There's a lot of pressure to look beautiful and trendy when you're a star. According to Taylor, this is the reason some celebrities feel bad about how they look and take drastic action to appear thinner or younger.

"I think the reason a lot of celebrities feel insecure and want to stop eating altogether is because they see

so many pictures of themselves on a daily basis," Taylor told *Glamour*. "It's unhealthy how many times you see your own image—it's just constant. When you see something enough, you're going to tear it down to the point where some days you feel like you're not even pretty."

So what feature does Taylor feel insecure about? Her eyes. She once read a blog that said her eyes were too small. "I thought, 'Are my eyes small? Oh no—they are!'" she recalled thinking.

That's right; even Taylor Swift feels bad about her looks from time to time. It's only natural, she said. "Everybody looks in the mirror and is like, 'I wonder why her eyes are huge and mine are smaller,'" she told *Seventeen*. "But I realized that if you're lucky enough to be different from everybody else, don't change."

Taylor soon realized the media's effect on her, and she took action to minimize negative feelings about herself. "I've stopped reading the comments below news articles and on gossip blogs because those are the ones that'll ruin your day in a second," she said. "You just have to be careful and filter the information you give yourself. Do you want to open the slam book today? Nope."

This attitude applies to comments about her music as well. Critics can be very heartless when judging the quality of music. "Some days you're just not confident, whether you have a platinum record or not—you read a bad review, or somebody has said something on a message board about you, and some days you believe it," she said. "And it's those days where I just have to recognize that it's one person, and they don't know me."

Instead of listening to other opinions, Taylor listens to herself. When it comes to keeping her slender figure, she listens to her body. "Basically, if I'm indulging too much, and not exercising enough, I can feel that," she said. "I can feel a change before I see it."

Taylor exercises when she can. She even has a treadmill on her tour bus so she can work out when it's convenient. For Taylor, exercise is a means of staying healthy, not a means of staying thin. "For me, working out is not so I can stay skinny. It's so that I can keep up my endurance, so I'm not panting on stage," she said. "Heavy breathing is the worst when you're in a concert. You don't want to see that, if you're going to see a show."

Hair Affair

■ In middle school, Taylor's friends made fun of her curls, and she straightened her hair to fit in with the cool crowd. But today, she embraces her naturally curly hair. She often wears her hair down, cascading over her shoulders. Here's her morning hair routine: "Wake up, touch up my curls with a spiral iron, and go," she said.

However, Taylor does wear her hair up from time to time. In the video for "Love Story" it's pinned up in a soft, romantic updo. It's a hairstyle women often request at salons for weddings and formal occasions.

Although she swore she'd never straighten her hair for a boy again, Taylor does straighten it from time to time for special occasions. When her hair is straight, it's sometimes pulled up into a sleek updo, like a French twist.

Has Taylor ever dyed her hair? No. She did, however, wear a brown wig for her appearance on *CSI* as well as her music video, "You Belong With Me."

Her craziest hair moment has to be the one featured on the cover of her *Fearless* album.

"At photo shoots, they blow wind at you all the time. It irritates my eyes, and I don't like it," she explained. "But the photographer put the wind on, like, hurricane mode. That's how we got that picture."

Chapter Eight

All Grown Up

Because Taylor Swift became an instant star after releasing her first hit single at age 16, she had to grow up in the public eye. She spent the remainder of her adolescence—the time when most teenagers mature into adulthood—in front of the camera. Everywhere she went, every boy she dated, every concert she gave, people were watching.

Taylor could have resented the attention, but instead, she welcomed it. Whether she was voting for the first time, putting together her first head-lining tour, or watching the nominations for an award show, Taylor remained candid about her thoughts and experiences. In fact, she often recorded these personal moments for her fans to see. As she transformed from a girl into a woman, the world watched in anticipation of her future, wondering what was in store for Taylor Swift.

The Right to Vote

In December 2007, Taylor turned 18 years old. By November of the following year, she was eligible to vote in her first presidential election. That election was one of the most politically charged races for the White House. At the time, current President George W. Bush had received public criticism for his management of Operation Iraqi Freedom, the war in Iraq. President Bush, a Republican, had served two terms and as Election Day approached, Americans began to argue about who would be his replacement. After a very long primary race, Arizona Senator John McCain was named the Republican candidate with running mate Alaska Governor Sarah Palin, and Illinois Senator Barack Obama was named the Democrat candidate with running mate Delaware Senator Joe Biden.

Voting in the 2008 presidential election was a huge honor for Taylor. "I'm really excited about having the opportunity to vote in this election," Taylor explained. "My friends and I talk about it all the time, about the candidates and the issues. It's still hard to imagine that when we cast our votes that they are actually going to count towards deciding who is going to be the next President of the United States. What we think and feel is going to count! The fact that our views matter is very empowering."

Taylor discussed her excitement about voting with the media, but she never shared which candidate she preferred. When asked if she was a Republican or a Democrat, she said, "I don't think I'm either."

Some famous actors or musicians get involved in politics and promote certain candidates. Taylor did not participate in any political events. "I just try and stick to my specialty, and my specialty is music and writing

Giving **Back**

■ Taylor may not have backed a specific candidate in the 2008 presidential election, but in 2007 she joined forces with Tennessee Governor Phil Bredesen on a worthwhile cause: fighting Internet sex predators. Many children and teens use the Internet for school assignments and keeping up with friends, but the Internet can be a dangerous place for kids. Sex predators use e-mail, chat rooms, and social networking sites to befriend kids and then lure them out of the home to meet them in person. Along with the Tennessee Association of Chiefs of Police, Taylor Swift joined the Governor in launching a statewide public education campaign called "Delete Online Predators."

Taylor served as a spokesperson for the campaign. "Chatting with friends and surfing the Internet is cool. But it's important to stay safe," she said. "Be smart about keeping your identity private online."

Taylor joined another good cause the following year. In June 2008, a large portion of Iowa near Iowa City and Cedar Rapids flooded when nearby rivers overflowed. Taylor helped by donating $100,000 to the Red Cross to aid relief efforts. When she performed in U.S. Cellular Center in downtown Cedar Rapids, the first show there after the flood occurred, Taylor projected pictures of the flood onstage via large screens to honor the people of Iowa and their quest to rebuild after the disaster.

songs," she explained. "I don't think it's my job to try and influence people which way they should vote, because it's a very personal thing."

Taylor paid attention to the candidates' debates and read articles about the election. "Honestly, I think it's good to be well versed on the election and who believes in what," she told *Rolling Stone*. "Sometimes, I think you can oversaturate yourself with facts, and in a lot of cases, it sounds cliché, but you should really just do what you feel."

Taylor listened to her feelings on Election Day 2008. "All the way through the line—I waited an hour and a half to vote—I was wavering back and forth whose ideas I liked better, and who really represented what I believed in," she said of her voting experience, which she recorded and posted on MySpace. "I kept going back over articles I'd read, and trying to figure out who to vote for. When I got in the voting booth, I just said to myself, 'All of my best decisions have been based on my gut instinct. Who's the President of the United States?' And, I pushed a name and I voted."

Although Taylor never divulged her choice, some journalists believed she hinted at voting for Barack Obama, the Democrat candidate who campaigned for change and won the election. "I've never seen this country so happy about a political decision in my entire time of being alive," Taylor said. "I'm so glad this was my first election."

Headlining Tour

Taylor released her sophomore album *Fearless* in November 2008 to rave reviews. Taylor actually co-produced

the album with Nathan Chapman, who produced Taylor's first album and many of her music videos. The *Fearless* CD jacket included pictures by photographer Anthony Baker, who shot scenes to match the theme of each song. For example, the lyrics to "You're Not Sorry" were accompanied by a photo of Taylor sitting on a bathroom floor surrounded by graffiti.

Like her self-titled album, all the songs on *Fearless* were inspired by Taylor's life. The CD included a song titled "Fearless," but according to Taylor, the album title was a statement about her approach to life. "I'm afraid of finding the most perfect love and losing it," she explained to *Girl's Life*. "I'm afraid of my career becoming mediocre and not being able to excite people anymore. I'm afraid of running out of things to write about. But I think there's something fearless about jumping, even though you're really scared of where you might land."

Taylor took a huge leap in January 2009 when she announced her *Fearless* Tour, the first headlining tour of her career. At age 19, Taylor

set off to play 52 concerts throughout the United States and the United Kingdom. Her fans were obviously ecstatic about the news. A month before her first concert in Edwardsville, Indiana, all 52 shows were sold out. Many of her concerts sold out in record time. Madison Square Garden in New York sold out in one minute, while The Staples Center in L.A. sold out in two minutes.

Taylor has toured in the past with country singers George Strait, Brad Paisley, Kenny Chesney, and the group Rascal Flatts. Taylor learned a lot from these veteran performers. "I've been on tour with every single one of my heroes, and I've seen what they do live," she said. "Some things have blown me away, and I've taken away some things that I really want to incorporate."

Of course, Taylor also wanted to try new things for her headlining tour. When she drew up a stage plan of what the production would look like, it didn't resemble the tours she'd accompanied in the past. "I feel like there's drama that I've always been attracted to—sort of a theatrical type,

> *"I've been on tour with every single one of my heroes, and I've seen what they do live," she said. "Some things have blown me away, and I've taken away some things that I really want to incorporate."*

dramatic performance that I feel is sometimes missing when you see shows these days," she told *Rolling Stone* before her tour began. "I never want people to think that they're just seeing a show where I'm playing song, after song, after song. When I play a song, I want people to feel like they're experiencing exactly what I

2009, she played a grand piano for the song "You're Not Sorry," to which she added a rendition of "What Goes Around ... Comes Around" by Justin Timberlake. She covered songs by Rihanna and Beyonce Knowles in concert too. While playing her song "Change" in Los Angeles, she showed footage of economic and natural di-

designed the stage, which included a hidden elevator and a room with racks of clothes for multiple costume changes. No decision was made without Taylor's input, according to her mother. "Every single decision that's made, whether it's talking about artwork that's going to go on the side of the buses for the tour or a script that needs to be read, you know, almost invariably, someone in the room says, 'Have you checked with Taylor?'" Andrea Swift said.

Taylor gave her band and crew a pep talk. "You're my brothers and my sisters, and I just want to thank you for that," she told them. "And I couldn't, I couldn't love you more. And we're going to go out there and be fearless."

went through when I wrote the song as I'm singing it for them."

Taylor added drama to her *Fearless* tour concerts through video footage, costume changes, six expert dancers, and special effects. For example, Taylor dressed up as Juliet when she sang "Love Story" and as a band member for "You Belong with Me." During "Should've Said No," Taylor and her fiddle player, Caitlin, banged on overturned garbage cans with drumsticks; one night, Taylor got so into the act, she cut her finger on the metal drum. "Should've Said No" is also the song Taylor sang under a cascading waterfall.

When Taylor performed back-to-back concerts in Chicago in October

sasters via an onstage screen. By the end of the song, positive and more hopeful images replaced the distressing ones.

All of Taylor's theatrical stunts and surprises are geared to make her fans' experience unique. That's Taylor goal whenever she tours. "If they want to hear the record, they'll listen to it. You know? They'll put in the CD or they'll listen to their iPod," she said. "But if they want to come out to a concert, I feel like it should be something completely different."

Putting a concert together is hard work, and Taylor was behind every aspect of her *Fearless* Tour, including the musical arrangements and transitions between songs. She even

Before taking her *Fearless* Tour on the road, Taylor, her band, and her crew practiced for three weeks in a secret warehouse in Nashville. However, she did allow *Dateline NBC* behind-the-scenes access for an episode titled "On Tour with Taylor Swift," which aired in May 2009. Their cameras shot never-before-seen footage of her warehouse and her stage. *Dateline* also captured rare moments on the actual tour. For instance, the night of Taylor's first *Fearless* Tour concert in Edwardsville, Indiana, Taylor got hot candle wax in her eye four hours before she was to be onstage. Fortunately, she recovered. Just before the show began, Taylor gave her band and crew a pep talk. "You're my brothers and my sisters, and I just want to thank you for that," she told them. "And I couldn't, I couldn't love you more. And we're going to go out there and be fearless."

Taylor didn't hit the road alone, of course. She invited great musical acts to open for her on tour, like her good friend Kellie Pickler, who rocked the stage every night with her tune "Didn't You Know How Much I Loved You." Kellie is known to sign autographs for fans while she's performing on stage. At a concert in Spokane,

> ## *"I can't even tell you how unreal it is for me, being up there, looking at those crowds. I just never thought I'd luck out like this."*

Washington, she even invited a girl celebrating her fifth birthday up on stage.

Taylor's other opening act was a four-member band named Gloriana, made up of musicans Tom Gossin, Mike Gossin, Rachel Reinert, and Cheyenne Kimball. "They're AMAZ-ING and I love their new single 'Wild at Heart,'" Taylor told her fans on MySpace. "I heard it and immediately knew I wanted them on this tour.... Everyone in Nashville is buzzing about them, and now I get to have them out with ME this summer."

Throughout her *Fearless* Tour, Taylor put her fans first and foremost. She did meet-and-greets before and after her concerts with people who won radio call-in shows or fans her crew discovered in the nosebleed section of the arena. Once, after going to bed at 3 AM one night after a concert, she got up only a few hours later to sign autographs for fans, people who had slept out on the street the night before just to meet her. Taylor's fans are, after all, the reason she loves playing concerts. "When I hear that high-pitched sound of all those people screaming together, it's like, I want to get on stage right now," said Taylor, who accompanied Keith Urban on his *Escape Together* World Tour while still headlining her own

tour. "It's the most amazing feeling. It's one of the craziest feelings to be on stage and know that you were sitting on your bedroom floor when that song came to be and now there's an arena full of people singing it."

Some musicians might be turned off by overemotional fans, but Taylor Swift loves when her fans get hysterical while she's on tour. "I love it when people get really excited," she told *The Oprah Winfrey Show* backstage. "I'm not afraid of people starting to cry and like losing their minds. I get excited about things when goods things happen. I just freak out. A lot of my fans are very excited about things too. So when they come through the meet and greet line, we have a lot of criers, and I like it."

While on tour, Taylor took time out of her busy schedule to surprise two of her fans on *The Oprah Winfrey Show*. In addition to saying hello to ten-year-old Jordan, Taylor also greeted Megan and Liz, twin sisters who not only cover Taylor's songs but also post their performances on the Internet. The twins went on Skype with the understanding they would discuss a possible appearance on *The Oprah Winfrey Show* with one of Oprah's producers. But really, their Skype video played on an actual show, where they got to say hello to

Taylor and learn fabulous news. The twins received tickets to Taylor's concert in Chicago; Oprah even sent a car to Michigan to drive them to the venue.

Throughout the tour, Taylor took breaks to make appearances like this or for other engagements, but her breaks were never long. She said she missed the tour, even when she was gone for only a day. "I've never had more fun doing anything in my life than I have on the *Fearless* Tour," she wrote on MySpace. "Thank you so much to everyone who has come to see the show. I can't even tell you how unreal it is for me, being up there, looking at those crowds. I just never thought I'd luck out like this."

The *Fearless* Tour was supposed to end in late November 2009, with several performances in the United Kingdom. But the tour was such a success, Taylor expanded it into the following year. In February 2010, Taylor planned to resume her tour in Brisbane, Australia, and continued to tour the United States and Canada through June 2010.

In addition to announcing her expanded tour, Taylor also re-released *Fearless* in late October 2009. The platinum edition two-disc set included six new songs, "Jump Then Fall," "Untouchable," "Come in with the Rain," "Superstar," "The Other Side of the Door" and a piano version of "Forever and Always." The CD/DVD combo also included music videos, behind the scenes footage, and exclusive photos of the *Fearless* Tour taken by Taylor's brother, Austin.

Thanks to the makers of Guitar Hero™, fans can also see Taylor Swift in concert on their home television. Taylor is one of several real-life musicians

Inside Taylor's
Tour Bus

■ For the first two years of her career, Taylor toured on a crowded bus with her band and crew. But due to her success, she was able to purchase her own tour bus. Her mom rides with her most of the time. Taylor said the bus was her biggest splurge, but it seems to be money well spent. "I feel like I'm home whenever I'm on my tour bus," she told JustJared.com.

Her tour bus certainly has a home-like feel. The "living room" boasts dark hardwood floors, comfy couches, a fireplace and a large flat screen television. The kitchen has a stainless steel refrigerator, while the bunk beds have pull-down televisions that recede into the ceiling above. Taylor actually designed the bus herself. "It was while I was making my second album, so when I would leave the studio I would go over to the bus place and help them design it," she explained to *Dateline NBC*.

When designing the bus, Taylor remembered the things she didn't have at home. "I'm so excited 'cause I've never had a TV in my room before until I got this bus," she explained. The bus even has a treadmill, which allows her to exercise without being photographed, something that might happen if she went to a gym.

"I just don't want to look nasty and sweaty when people are taking pictures of me," she said.

No tour bus would be complete without Taylor's favorite number, 13. She put the number on the tour bus door and touches it every night before she goes on stage.

The tour bus is not the only place for Taylor to feel at home while on the road. Backstage, she also has a clubhouse that's called the "T Party" room. It boasts a ping-pong table, foosball table, and big-screen TV. "It's a room I've always wanted to have on other tours. It looks nothing like backstage. It looks like your living room," Taylor said. "The walls are covered in magenta/maroon/gold/purple draped fabric, and the floors are carpeted with oriental rugs on top. There are lanterns hanging from the ceiling and candles everywhere. In the middle of everything is a column with pictures of my band and me all over it. Pictures that remind me of home."

who appear virtually in Band Hero™, released in November 2009. Music and videogame enthusiasts can play as Taylor, or beside her, on songs like "Love Story," "You Belong with Me," and "Picture to Burn."

"Anything that encourages people to pick up an instrument and play, I'm fully behind. And, I'm really excited about Band Hero™, because not only are fans getting to play my songs, but I'm actually in the game," explained Taylor. "It's so cool for people to feel like they are experiencing one of my concerts. This is one of the closest things out there to going to see me perform!"

Taylor's Future

What does the future hold for Taylor Swift? Certainly the release of more successful albums. By the fall of 2009, she had written many songs for a third album and had recorded about half of them. She'll continue to collaborate with the excellent songwriters she's worked with in the past, like Liz Rose, Hillary Lindsey and John Rich. Although she's sold over 10 million units of her music, including all of her albums and online sales, there is more for Taylor to conquer. She still wants to do a world tour.

So where does Taylor see herself in 10 years? She's not fearful of the future, but she's uncertain where she'll be. "I could have kids," she told *Dateline NBC*. "I could be married. I could be single. I could—I could live in Nashville, or I could live in L.A., or I could live in the Bahamas. I don't know...if you would have told me four years ago that I'd be sitting here, you know, putting together this huge tour and winning album of the year, I wouldn't have believed you. And to think ten years from now, that's such a long time. And I'm just open to whatever it brings."

There is one thing Taylor Swift knows about the future. She'll still love music. She hopes to be touring still in 10 or 20 years. "I'd love to always be present in music, writing songs, but I'm not the kind of person who will hang around if I become irrelevant," she said. "I'll bow out gracefully, raise my kids and have a garden. And I'm going to let my hair go gray when I'm older—I don't need to be blond when I'm 60."

Her colleagues believe she has a lengthy career ahead of her. "Taylor will be around a long time," predicted country singer Brad Paisley "Her audience will grow with her."

This is exactly what Taylor wants. She believes she's still the same person she was when she started out, but admitted that as her life changes, her music will change with it. But she never wants to change too much that her fans ever feel abandoned. She won't forget that country music helped her rise to fame. "My fans are so important to me, and I would love for them to grow up with me," she said. "But I never want to throw anyone for a loop or change so much that people can't recognize me.... I'm looking forward to experiencing more in life and being able to translate that into new songs."

No matter what the future holds, Taylor said she would remain appreciative of her success and never allow herself to become complacent. "I continue to walk around with the mentality that I'm not really a big deal because as fast as it came, it can go," she told the *Reading Eagle*.

For that reason, she said she's never going to feel she's at the top of her game. "All of this is amazing, but it doesn't guarantee anything about the future," she told *Teen Vogue*. "I still haven't made it to where I want to be."

A Place of Her Own

Once, when discussing her future, Taylor mentioned she'd like to move out of her parents' house one day. Well, that day finally came. After Taylor bought a condominium in Nashville, she announced the news about her new place in September 2009, while chatting with the ladies on *The View*.

Before moving, Taylor spent a lot of time designing and decorating her new condo to make it feel like home. In the past, she imagined she'd have a hard time making interior design choices. "You know when you walk into a furniture store, and you're like, 'Oh, that's how I'm going to decorate my house,' and then the next one you're like, 'No, that's going to be the way I decorate my house?'" she told *Rolling Stone*. "I think when I do it, I'm going to be so indecisive."

But it seemed Taylor wasn't indecisive at all. Taylor gave details about her new place when she visited *The Oprah Winfrey Show* in October of 2009. "All I talk about now is tiles and paint and stuff," she told Oprah.

Taylor said she wanted her condo to have an "Old World, eclectic feel," one that would boast "a different knob on every cabinet." Taylor also said she loves bright colors and draping fabrics. She would fill the condo with antiques she bought during her travels.

And, perhaps to prove she's still a kid at heart, she said she wanted a

tree house in her living room.

Pajama Party

Watching the 2009 Country Music Awards nominations was a big moment for Taylor Swift, and she shared her reaction to the news with her fans. On her MySpace page, she posted a video of herself watching the nominations

The video was set to the song "Love Story" and showed Taylor sitting in her pajamas on a bed with her mom, who seemed to wear PJs as well. It was a family affair; both of Taylor's dogs were in bed too. They had gotten up early to watch the nominations on television. "It's 8:30 AM, but it's worth it," Taylor said to the video camera. "I'm really nervous and excited."

Taylor crossed her fingers and even wiggled in her seat as she waited to hear her name. She held on to one of the dogs to steady herself. She clapped for other "Female Vocalist of the Year" nominees, but when she heard her name, she screamed and hoisted her arm into the air in victory before giving her mom a high five. More outbursts occurred after hearing she was up for "Music Video of The Year" and "Album of the Year," but her biggest reaction came when she was named a nominee for "Entertainer of the Year." She showed her enthusiasm by rolling around on the bed and kicking her feet.

Taylor then proceeded to call her dad to tell him the news. "My stomach hurts so bad," she told him.

SNL, CMAs and More Honors

The fall of 2009 proved to be a very busy season for Taylor Swift. At

Dream **Duets**

■ Taylor loves to perform solo, but collaborating with another musician makes her job twice as fun. For instance, she sang alongside Colbie Caillat in "Breathe" on her *Fearless* album. Taylor has mentioned a number of singers with whom she'd liked to collaborate, like Kenny Chesney or Garth Brooks. "I look up to them so much for their work ethic," she told CMT News. "I was lucky enough to open up for Kenny on some shows...watching him work was so inspiring. He and Garth just represent true artists to me, and any project I could work with one of them would be an honor."

For a long time, Taylor also wanted to work with John Mayer, and her wish finally came true. Taylor and John sang together when she performed at The Staples Center in Los Angeles in 2009. The two sang "Your Body is a Wonderland" and "White Horse" together. But Taylor never imagined they'd do a duet together for a CD.

"He Twittered the other day that he wrote a song and he wants to make it a duet with me," Taylor told *Elle*. "I freaked out when I heard, because I've been such a big fan of John for such a long time. I'm really excited about just the idea that he would even mention me in his Twitter!"

Of course, Taylor said yes to the invitation. The song, "Half of my Heart," appeared on John Mayer's album *Battle Studies*, released in November 2009.

Taylor said she'd be honored to sing a duet with Garth Brooks.

the end of October, she performed two songs on an episode of *Dancing with the Stars*. She then made another appearance on *The Ellen DeGeneres Show*, where she presented Ellen with a five million worldwide sales plaque. After all, it was on Ellen's show that Taylor kicked off the release of her *Fearless* album. During her visit, Taylor also co-wrote a song with Ellen, which featured the day's secret word "spiral staircase."

On November 7, Taylor continued making television performances when she served as both host and musical guest of *Saturday Night Live*. The *SNL* producers had asked Taylor to host during the summer, so she had to keep the "mind-blowing" news a secret until that fall. "I've been thinking about skit ideas for a long time," Taylor explained to the *Tennessean* before the show aired.

"There are definitely some hilarious things that have happened to me over the past couple of months that I think will be pretty substantial skits."

On *SNL*, Taylor performed two of her songs, the well-known "You Belong with Me" and one of her newer songs, "Untouchable." She began the evening with a monologue—sung to a tune, of course—that listed all of the things she would not discuss in her monologue. These topics included her affinity for glitter, her phone call breakup with Joe Jonas, the Kanye West incident, and whether she was dating actor Taylor Lautner. Relationship rumors were circling at the time after photos of the two Taylors—on a date in Beverly Hills—had surfaced on the Internet. Neither of the Taylors had verified or denied the rumors, but Taylor certainly acted smitten during her song. "And if you're wondering if I might/be dating the werewolf from *Twilight*," Taylor sang in her monologue, before pausing to mouth "Hi, Taylor" and blow a kiss at the screen. "I'm not going to talk about that in my monologue."

Because she appeared in most of the comedy sketches, Taylor demonstrated her ability to not only sing, but also act. In a spoof of the show *The View*, she played guest host Kate Gosselin of the reality show *Jon & Kate Plus 8*. Wearing a fun wig matching Kate's unique hairstyle, Taylor acted the part well. She also played a lip-biting Kristen Stewart-like character in a trailer for a film called *Firelight*, a spoof of the *Twilight* movie featuring a family of Frankensteins instead of vampires. Other skits included Taylor playing a teen named Samantha Sanders, founder of Teens Raising Awareness About Awful Parent Driving; a local convict with cornrows and a goatee; and even Latin singer Shakira in a spoof of her song, "Hips Don't Lie"

Taylor received good reviews about her appearance on *SNL*, which attracted about five million viewers. *Entertainment Weekly* said she "proved to be this season's best *Saturday Night Live* host so far. Admirably resilient in a wide variety of

sketch roles.... Swift was always up for the challenge, seemed to be having fun, and helped the rest of the cast nail the punch lines." *Rolling Stone* also praised Taylor's performance, saying she "...did a masterful job in both roles, appearing in nearly all the sketches."

Just a few days after the *SNL* appearance, Taylor won Song of the Year for "Love Story" at the 57th Annual BMI Country Awards. She had won the same award the year before for "Teardrops on My Guitar." The very next day, November 11, she attended the 43rd annual Country Music Association Awards, where she was up for four major awards, all voted on by fans. On the big day, Taylor posted this update on Twitter: "Getting all pumped up for the CMAs, blasting Timbaland, 'Morning after Dark' in the dressing room. PARTY!"

Before the award show began, during a special off-air ceremony, Taylor won her first award of the evening for Music Video of the Year for "Love Story." Soon after, she started the live award show with an emphatic performance of "Forever & Always." Before she broke out into song, a video played of Taylor being interviewed by Nancy O'Dell of *Access Hollywood*. Nancy first noted how Taylor worked the names of her ex-boyfriends into her songs. "Aren't you afraid that by writing those songs that you're going to scare off guys from dating you?" Nancy asked.

"I just figure that if guys don't want me to write bad songs about them, then they shouldn't do bad things," Taylor replied.

This response echoed through Sommet Center in Downtown Nash-

ville and set off her live, feisty performance of "Forever & Always," the song she wrote about ex-boyfriend, Joe Jonas. Taylor, who wore black leather pants and a black, billowy-sleeved blouse, added drama to her routine by throwing a chair off a platform and sliding down a metal pole. She even sang part of the song on her knees, with her hair blown around her face by a wind machine.

Later that night, the award show hosts, Brad Paisley and Carrie Underwood, could not resist spoofing the Kanye West Video Music Awards debacle. While Brad Paisley made an impromptu acceptance speech about his video "Welcome to the Future," an old man in a large cowboy hat barged on stage to say, "I know you had a nice video and all that, but Taylor Swift made the best video of all time." This skit made the crowd roar in applause and caused Taylor Swift to smile and clutch her chest in laughter.

Taylor accepted her second award of the night for Album of the Year, "Fearless." "This album is my diary, and so to all the people who voted for me for this, thank you for saying that you like my diary," Taylor said in her acceptance speech. "Cause that's the nicest thing, the nicest compliment." Taylor went on to thank her fans, her band members, and the two men sitting in the audience who believed in her, Scott Borchetta and her father, Scott Swift.

Soon after, Taylor performed her second song of the evening, "Fifteen." This time, she performed with less flair, sitting on a stool in the middle of the crowd while playing acoustic guitar. She seemed carefree wearing a purple dress and cowboy boots. The

After winning Entertainer of the Year at the 2009 CMAs, Taylor shared a group hug with her band.

fans surrounding her, some of them Henderson High School students, sang along with the song's chorus and held huge signs that read, "I love TS."

It wasn't long before Taylor was on stage again, accepting her third award for Female Vocalist of the Year. "I hope you know how much this means to me," she said. "I want to thank country radio. You guys started taking chances on me, playing my music a few short years ago." She also thanked Reba McEntire and Faith Hill for being themselves, and every person in the arena for not "running up on the stage during this speech."

Taylor may have been joking about Kanye West during that acceptance speech, but her next speech was full of tears. Overcome by emotion, Taylor could barely speak when she was named Entertainer of the Year, the biggest and last award of the evening.

Taylor was the youngest recipient of the prestigious award. "I will never forget this moment because in this moment, everything that I have ever wanted has just happened to me," she exclaimed. She then welcomed her band members to the stage to share in her joy. They all engaged in a group hug. In the audience, her father's eyes were also full of tears.

Of course, Taylor once again thanked her fans. "And the fans who come to the shows with your shirts that you made yourself and the looks on your face, that's why I do this," she said. "Thank you for this moment. Thank you."

She did not forget to thank her competition as well, the four men also nominated for Entertainer of the Year: Kenny Chesney, Brad Paisley, George Strait and Keith Urban. "Every single person in that category

let me open up for them this year," Taylor said. "Thank you so much y'all. I love you."

After the CMAs, on November 22, Taylor rounded out the month by performing at the 37th annual American Music Awards, where she was nominated for six awards in both country and pop/rock categories. These included Artist of the Year, Country Favorite Female Artist, Country Favorite Album "Fearless," Pop/Rock Favorite Album "Fearless," Pop/Rock Favorite Female Artist, and Adult Contemporary Favorite Artist. Taylor was also nominated for three People's Choice Awards, including Favorite Country Artist, Favorite Pop Artist, and Favorite Female Artist. The show was to air in January 2010, kicking off another year of possibilities for the beautiful, talented Taylor Swift.

BIBLIOGRAPHY

Online & Print Articles

Bonajuro, Alison. "Taylor Swift at Allstate Arena." *Chicago Tribune*. 12 Oct. 2009.

Bried, Erin. "Taylor Swift has 1,056,375 friends." *Self*. Mar. 2009: 44-46.

Caramanica, John. "A Young Outsider's Life..." *The New York Times*. 5 Sept. 2008.

Corbett, Holly. "Taylor Swift: She won't run..." *Seventeen*. May 2009: 108, 111-112.

Day, Rick. "10 Questions for Taylor Swift." *Time* 23. April 2009.

DeMara, Bruce. "Taylor Swift: Country music's rising star." *The Star*. 12 Jan. 2008.

Ditzian, Eric. "Taylor Swift Goes Cinderella..." *MTV*. 13 Sept. 2009.

Evans, Rory. "Taylor Made." *Women's Health*. Dec. 2008.

Finan, Eileen. "Guy Behind Taylor Swift Song Revealed." *People*. 2 Dec. 2008.

Finan, Eileen. "Taylor Swift Goes to Prom." *People*. 21 April 2008.

Freedom du Lac, J. "Taylor Swift...Kid in Country." *The Washington Post*. 28 Feb 2008.

Forr, Amanda. "Fabulously Fearless." *Girl's Life* Dec 2008/Jan. 2009: 50-52.

Grigoriadis, Vanessa. "Taylor Swift in Her Own Words" *Rolling Stone*. 20 Feb. 2009

Grigoriadis, Vanessa. "The Very Pink, Very Perfect Life..." *Rolling Stone*. 19 Feb 2009.

Hatza, George. "Taylor Swift: Growing into superstardom." *Reading Eagle*. 12 Dec 2008.

Horner, Marianne. "Taylor Swift: Letting Her Hair Down." *Country Weekly*. 12 Jan 2009.

Keel, Beverly. "Wait a minute, says Tim..." *The Tennessean*. 21 Aug 2006

Kotb, Hoda. "On tour with Taylor Swift" *Dateline NBC*, Transcript 31 May 2009.

Mansfield, Brian; Freydkin, Donna; and Keveney, Bill. "Coming attractions: Not all boys make Taylor Swift cry." *USA Today*. 8 Aug. 2008.

Mansfield, Brian. "On the Verge: Taylor Swift." *USA Today*. 21 Nov. 2006: 5.

Mansfield, Brian. "Teen hops on back of Tim McGraw." *USA Today*. 20 Nov. 2006.

McCafferty, Dennis. "Taylor's Swift Rise" *USA Weekend*. 13 April 2008.

McKay, Holly. "Taylor Swift Snaps over Miley Cyrus." *Fox News*. 27 May 2008

Merkin, Daphne. "The Story Teller." *Allure*. April 2009: 188, 190, 192-193, 196.

Montes, Michael. "Interview, Taylor Swift." *Florida Entertainment Scene*. 17 July 2007.

Pareles, John. "She's a Little Bit Country..." *The New York Times*. 28 Aug. 2009.

Pellettieri, Cortney. "Taylor Swift: On My Mind." *InStyle*. July 2009: 182.

Rasmussen, Tracy. "Berks native Taylor Swift's..." *Reading Eagle*. 8 Feb 2008.

Regan, Kayla. "Taylor Swift visits University." *The Kansan*. 28 April 2009

Rieckhoff, Sydney. "The Fearless Taylor Swift." *Scholastic*. 10 Nov. 2008.

Rosen, Craig. "Taylor Swift Concert Review." *Hollywood Reporter*. 26 May 2009.

Rosen, Jody. "Taylor Swift: Little Miss Perfect" *Blender*. 6 March 2008.

Rosenberg, Carissa. "...This Girl is Singing Your Song." *Seventeen*. June 2008: 98-101.

Sandell, Laurie. "Taylor Swift: Bomb-Shell in Blue Jeans." *Glamour*. 1 July 2009.

Scaggs, Austin. "Q & A: Taylor Swift." *Rolling Stone*. 27 Nov. 2008.

Scaggs, Austin. "The Unabridged Taylor Swift." *Rolling Stone*. 2 Dec. 2008.

"Taylor Swift: Cover Spy." *Cosmo Girl*. Dec. 2008/Jan. 2009: 18.

"Taylor Swift: The Phenomenon." *Cosmo Girl*. Dec. 2008/Jan. 2009: 101-105.

Tucker, Ken. "Taylor Swift Goes Global." *Billboard*. 25 Oct. 2008: 22-25.

Vadnal, Julie. "Women in Music: Taylor Swift." *Elle*. 15 June 2009.

Vena, Jocelyn. "Miley Cyrus Calms Taylor Swift's Grammy Nerves." *MTV*. 8 Feb. 2009

Vena, Jocelyn. "Taylor Swift Admires Rihanna's VMA Style." *MTV*. 13 Sept. 2009

Vena, Jocelyn. "Taylor Swift Announces New Leg of Fearless Tour." *MTV*. 8 Oct. 2009.

Vena, Jocelyn. "Taylor Swift 'Shocked' by VMA Nod..." *MTV*. 2 Sept. 2008.

Waterman, Laura. "Swift Ascent." *Teen Vogue*. March 2009.

Willman, Chris. "American Girl." *Entertainment Weekly*. 8 Feb. 2008: 40-43.

Willman, Chris. "Swift Rise." *Entertainment Weekly*. 20 Sept. 2009.

"5 Question for Taylor Swift." *People*. 1 Dec. 2008: 36.

"20 Question with Taylor Swift" *CMT News*. 12 Nov 2007. 22 Sept. 2009.

Data, Images & Video Clips Accessed at the Following Websites:

http://www.bbc.co.uk/blogs
http://www.bmi.com
http://www.checkitoutmusic.com
http://www.cmt.com
http://www.countrystandardtime.com
http://ellen.warnerbros.com
http://www.facebook.com
http://www.farmersalmanac.com/
http://www.gactv.com/
http://www.georgestrait.com/
http://www.glamour.com
http://hub.guitarhero.com/games/bh
http://www.theinsider.com
http://justinemagazine.com/taylor.
http://justjared.buzznet.com
http://www.looktothestars.org
http://www.myspace.com
http://www.musicrow.com
http://www.msnbc.msn.com
http://www.mtv.com
http://www.myspace.com/taylorswift
http://www.oceanup.com
http://www.oprah.com
http://www.seventeen.com
http://www.taylorswift.com
http://www.vh1.com/
http://www.youtube.com/

Interviews

Luyben, Sharon, former music teacher of Taylor Swift. Personal interview. 2 Sept. 2009.